Merry Christ—
Rose

You're a very special person
Nancy

His
Mysterious
Ways

A treasury of inspiring stories from the pages of Guideposts

His Mysterious Ways

Compiled by the Editors

WORD PUBLISHING
Dallas · London · Sydney · Singapore

All Scripture quotations, unless otherwise noted, are from the King
James or Authorized Version of the Bible.

Scripture quotations marked RSV are from the Revised Standard Ver-
sion of the Bible, copyright 1946, 1952, 1971 by the Division of Christian
Education of the National Council of the Churches of Christ in the
United States of America, and are used by permission.

Scripture quotations marked NIV are from the New International Version of the Bible, copyright © 1978 by New York International Bible
Society, and are used by permission.

Scripture quotations marked TLB are from *The Living Bible,* copyright
1971 owned by transfer to Illinois Marine Bank N.A. (as trustee). Used
by permission of Tyndale House Publisher, Wheaton, IL 60188.

"My Sailor Boy," by Ada Adams, as told to Phyllis Sjoblom (pp. 23-24),
is reprinted by permission of Phyllis Sjoblom and *The Pentecostal Evan-
gel.* Copyright © 1985 by the General Council of the Assemblies of
God.

Every attempt has been made to credit the sources of copyrighted
material used in this book. If any such acknowledgment has been
inadvertently omitted or miscredited, receipt of such information
would be appreciated.

All material appeared originally in *Guideposts* magazine. Copyright ©
1948, 1959, 1960, 1961, 1963, 1964, 1965, 1966, 1967, 1968, 1969, 1972,
1973, 1974, 1975, 1976, 1977, 1978, 1979, 1980, 1981, 1982, 1983, 1984,
1985, 1986, 1987.

Contents

Introduction

Year in year out, "His Mysterious Ways" has remained the most popular regular feature in *Guideposts* magazine. That makes sense in a way, for what reader is there who doesn't love a good mystery? I remember the time, however, when readers would send in their reports of "mysterious" spiritual happenings and we who edit the magazine would send them back, gratefully and with regret. They simply did not seem to fit into our format.

Guideposts was created almost half a century ago to help people. From the beginning the magazine has called itself "A Practical Guide to Successful Living," and in its pages ordinary and extraordinary people have told how they have applied practical spiritual tools in overcoming life's most difficult trials. But when the mail would bring in a manuscript about a man dying of thirst on a broiling hot desert, what practical spiritual tool was being employed when suddenly, out from a sunny, cloudless sky fell a deluge of life-giving hail? Who could explain those stories of strange signs appearing unsolicited from nowhere, the screams for help that were heard yet never uttered? Fascinating, yes, but too far beyond comprehension to be helpful to those of us leading undramatic lives in the day-to-day.

Then, one historic morning, someone said to us, "Why bother to explain those odd stories? If they happened, if they're true, why not just *believe* them? After all, isn't that the essence of faith?"

Those remarks heralded the beginning of the monthly feature "His Mysterious Ways." We saw that we could offer our readers no greater help than to remind them again and again that God reigns in this world, that our faith in Him requires no explanation. Indeed, faith is made of mystery and awe; it is not in knowing the tangible but in believing in the intangible that our faith flourishes. And so, in these stories collected from the pages of *Guideposts,* I hope that your faith, too, will be strengthened as you sense the hidden hand of God moving silently, leaving behind the evidence of things unseen.

—*Van Varner,*
Editor
Guideposts magazine

GOD
SPEAKS

The heavens declare the glory of God;
and the firmament sheweth his handiwork.
　　　　　　　　　　—Psalm 19:1

One thing God has spoken,
　two things I have heard:
that you, O God, are strong,
　and that you, O Lord, are loving.
　　　　　　　　—Psalm 62:11–12, NIV

In the Bible we have the record of God's speaking to His people in many varied ways. The Psalmist heard God's voice all around him—in the spring floods, the storms, the hills covered with green grass. The prophet Balaam even heard God speak through a donkey!

Today, if we will open our ears and eyes to receive His messages, we too can hear Him. "God is speaking all the time," missionary-educator Frank Laubach used to say. The people who share their stories with us were able to hear Him speak when they needed comfort or help. They were able to receive His directions to find and minister to people in need.

How does God speak? As you read *His Mysterious Ways* you'll discover He communicates through little things like a sparrow or a radio. Through coincidence, dreams, signs, impressions. Through strange things, like the cross in the water that led a pilot to the crew of a capsized boat. And through Scripture.

The stories also show us that when we receive a message we have to do something about it. The missionary mother in war-torn China, facing the threat of invading troops, found that the Scripture verses on her calendar, selected over a year before in England, gave her specific directions each day. Because she believed they were meant for her and did what they told her to, she and her children were kept from harm. When we hear God's voice and obey it, we will see His mysterious power at work.

His Eye Is on the Sparrow

Did you ever have the curious sensation that God was speaking to you? Not out loud but with some beautiful, out-of-the-way gesture?

I had that feeling at a memorial service for my dear octogenarian friend Elisabeth Moore. This wonderful woman had lost her husband very soon after their wedding, and in all the years after that she never remarried. She dedicated her whole life to caring for people who needed her, especially children whom she liked to pretend she "adopted."

At one point in the service, the organ played "His Eye Is on the Sparrow," and as a soloist began to sing, a tiny sparrow flew in through an open window. Three times it circled the church ceiling, and then flew out. The sight of it caused my skin to tingle. To me it seemed that the Lord was using that sparrow to tell us that He, too, was well pleased with the lovely Elisabeth. I felt a sense of awe.

Only later, talking to one of her "adopted" children, now grown, did I learn that "His Eye Is on the Sparrow" was Elisabeth's favorite song. But, checking back, we discovered that no one had requested it to be sung. It was just coincidence that the organist had chosen it.

Coincidence?

—*Josephine Novello*

The Heart-Shaped Tassel

Hearts. My mother always had a special thing about hearts. When I had chicken pox as a child, I remember her cheering me with heart-shaped peanut butter sandwiches. For years she embroidered heart designs on Raggedy Ann dolls to give away. Hearts were her gift of love, especially in difficult times.

And so, when my niece Laura was born with a serious physical defect and was fighting for her life, I wasn't surprised to find Mama in the waiting room, quietly sewing a tiny valentine heart onto a rag doll. I knew Mama was suffering. I even remembered her saying once that she couldn't bear the thought of a grandchild dying.

I prayed that day for little Laura, but I also prayed, "Please, Lord, be with Mama, too."

Weeks passed with no improvement in Laura's health, or in Mama's spirits. At last my parents decided to visit their country farm. I pictured the little gray farmhouse nestled under the big, spreading pecan tree, and I hoped that there Mama might find peace. A day later my phone rang. It was Mama. She asked me if I remembered how in June the pecan tree always shed its stringy seed tassels. I said I did.

Mama then said, "You know how badly I've needed to feel God's closeness. Well, Daddy and I were about to sweep the tassels off the porch when we looked down, and there I noticed one tassel in particular. Just guess how it was shaped."

Before I could guess, Mama joyously exclaimed, "It was in the perfect shape of a heart!"

—Sue Monk Kidd

Tuning In

I turn a dial
And here it is:
The light, the music,
Voices—more,
Never seen
Or heard before.

Now suddenly
I am aware
That YOU are here
Are everywhere—
God, around,
Above, within . . .
My only need
To tune You in.

—Mildred N. Hoyer

The Echo in the Radio

When our church observed "Women in the Pulpit Sunday," I was asked to give the morning sermon. In college I had enjoyed competing on our debating team, so I was used to speaking in front of people, but talking to my own congregation about faith made me unsure of myself. How could I find a way to convey my convictions?

I chose for my text Galatians 5:22–23: "But the fruit of the Spirit is love, joy, peace, longsuffering, gentleness, goodness, faith, meekness, temperance." I wanted to show how when we are close to God, when we truly tune in to Him, we can feel His love working through us and the "fruit of the Spirit" becomes a part of us. In preparation, I prayed earnestly for God's help in finding a simple way to make my point clear.

Then I got an inspiration. I took my twelve-year-old son's small transistor radio with me to the pulpit that Sunday morning. Near the end of my sermon I turned it on and held it up to the microphone. Since I had deliberately set the dial between two stations, loud, fuzzy static blasted through the speakers.

Pulling it away from the mike, I said, "That's what it's like when we're not living close to God. But when we're in tune with Him, we demonstrate love, joy, peace, longsuffering, gentleness, goodness, faith, meekness and temperance."

At that moment I turned the radio dial to the nearest station to demonstrate the clarity of a properly tuned-in radio. And out came a man's voice intoning words that proved my point better than anything that I myself could possibly have said: ". . . love, joy, peace, longsuffering, gentleness, goodness, faith, meekness, temperance."

—*Sharon L. Markle*

The Daily Miracle We Take for Granted

Darkness fades.
The fleecy mist recedes
Into the vastness of the sky
And leaves the landscape cool and crisp.
But moisture clings.
The tender grass is jewel-dressed with dew;
It gleams like diamonds on the spider's web
And strings the foliage of trees
With shining pearls.
The silence is complete, yet seems to speak:
Be still.
It's dawn.
Be still
And know that I am God.

—Leif Ingebregtsen

The Woman with the Umbrella

On a gloomy day years ago, my sister and I were driving back
home on the old Columbia River Highway. As we went past
the beautiful Multnomah Falls near Larch Mountain, Elva said
suddenly, "How odd. Why is that woman sitting there with an
umbrella? It isn't raining."

"What woman?" I said. I had seen no one. I thought Elva
must have dozed off and dreamed it.

"She was sitting on the ground beside the road, her feet out
in front of her, looking straight ahead," Elva insisted.

At home, we heard on TV that two hikers were lost on Larch
Mountain. "I'm *sure* I saw one of those women," Elva kept
saying, until finally we called the sheriff's office. That afternoon, two officers came and asked us to drive with them to the
place where Elva had seen the woman. We arrived at Multnomah Falls at dusk. Sheriff Terry Schrunk said that Elva's
description jibed perfectly with one of the women, even to the
umbrella and the color of her clothes. The police searched into
the darkness, then said they'd continue in the morning.

We went home. We prayed hard for the lost hikers and heard on the news that scores of other people were doing the same.

At 10:00 A.M., Sheriff Schrunk called—the women had been found! "They were on the mountain right above where your sister said we should look," he told me. "They were trapped above the falls."

"Trapped"—the women had been trapped, he said. They couldn't climb down. That meant there was no way that Elva could have seen one of them sitting beside the highway . . . !

—*Sylvia W. Stevens*

The Hearse in the Snow

My mother had been haunted by the same dream for five nights in a row. She described it to me as I took her to the hospital for an operation to relieve a slipped disk.

"It's snowing," she said. "In the distance I can see headlights approaching. When they come close, I recognize a hearse. It stops in front of me. A door opens and the driver motions me inside . . ."

Against her wishes, I told Mom's doctors and nurses about the dream so they would be sensitive to her fears about the operation.

Before dawn on the day of her surgery, snow began to fall. At 7:15 I went to her hospital room to be with her while she was being prepped. An orderly came in and I helped him get Mom on the gurney. We were waiting at the elevator when a nurse hurried up. "The surgery has been canceled," she said.

Finally I was able to reach our doctor to find out what was going on.

"Well, I woke up during the night and couldn't go back to sleep," he said. "Something was bothering me. I looked outside and saw the snow. And I thought about your mother's dream. I got up, called the hospital and ordered a second electrocardiogram. It caught a condition that didn't show up on the first EKG. The lab called the anesthesiologist and he canceled the procedure." The doctor hesitated and took a deep breath.

"If your mother had had the anesthesia, well . . ."

Later I found out what he did not say then. Under anesthesia, Mom would have been in grave danger of dying of heart failure.

—*June Davis, R.N.*

The Dream That Wouldn't Go Away

Back when I was a young livestock rancher north of Roosevelt, Utah, the news one cold November morning reported that a California doctor and his wife were missing on a flight from Custer, South Dakota, to Salt Lake City. As a student pilot, I had just completed my first cross-country flight with an instructor, though I had only twenty solo hours.

Paying close attention to all radio reports on the search, I was very disturbed two days later by a newscast saying that Dr. Robert Dykes and his wife, Margery, both in their late twenties and parents of two young children, were not likely to be found until spring—and maybe not even then. They had been missing four days, and the temperature had been below zero every night. There seemed little chance for their survival without food and proper clothing.

That night before I retired I said a simple prayer for these two people I didn't know. "Dear God, if they're alive, send someone to them so they will be able to get back to their family."

After a while I drifted off to sleep. In a dream I saw a red plane on a snow-swept ridge and two people waving for help. I awoke with a start. *Was it the Dykeses? What color was their plane?* I didn't remember any of the news reports ever mentioning it.

I couldn't get back to sleep for some time. I kept reasoning that because I'd been thinking of the couple before falling asleep, it was natural for me to dream them. When I finally did go to sleep, the dream came again! A red plane on a ridge—

but now farther away. I could still see two people waving, and could now see some snow-covered mountain peaks in the background.

I got out of bed and spread out the only air chart I owned. It covered a remote area in Utah—the High Uintas region, along the Wyoming-Utah border. The Dykeses' flight plan presumably had to pass over this range. I was familiar with the rugged terrain, for I had fished and hunted it as a boy. My eyes scanned the names on the chart—Burrow Peak, Painters Basin, Kings Peak, Gilbert Peak.

Again I went to bed. And again, incredibly, the dream returned! Now the plane was barely in sight. I could see a valley below. Then it came to me in a flash—Painters Basin and Gilbert Peak! I rose in a cold sweat. It was daylight.

Turning on the news, I found there had been no sign of the plane and the search had been called off. All that day, doing chores around the ranch, I could think of nothing but the Dykeses and my dream. I felt God had shown me where those people were and that they were alive. But who would believe me and what could I do about it? I knew I wasn't really qualified to search for them myself. I knew, too, that even trying to explain my dream to my flight instructor, a stern taskmaster named Joe Mower, would have me laughed out of the hangar.

I decided to go to our small rural airport anyway. When I arrived, a teenaged boy who was watching the place told me Joe had gone to town for the mail.

The force that had been nudging me all morning seemed to say, "Go!" I had the boy help me push an Aeronca plane out. When he asked where I was going, I said, "To look for the Dykeses." I gave the plane the throttle and was on my way.

Trimming out, I began a steady climb and headed for Uinta Canyon. I knew what I was doing was unwise, even dangerous, but the danger seemed a small thing compared to what I felt in my heart.

As I turned east near Painters Basin, I was beginning to lose faith in my dream; there was no sign of the missing plane. The high winds, downdrafts and rough air were giving me trouble in the small sixty-five-horsepower plane. Terribly disappointed as well as frightened, I was about to turn back when suddenly there it was! A red plane on Gilbert Peak, just as I had seen in my dream.

Coming closer, I could see two people waving. I was so happy I began to cry. "Thank You, God," I said over and over.

Opening the plane's window, I waved at the Dykeses and wigwagged my wings to let them know I saw them. Then I said a prayer to God to help me get back to the airport safely.

Thirty minutes later I was on the ground. When I taxied up and cut the motor, I gulped, for Joe Mower was there to greet me.

"You're grounded," he hollered. "You had no permission to take that plane up."

"Joe," I said quickly, "I know I did wrong, but listen, I found the Dykeses and they need help."

"You're crazy," Joe said, and he continued to yell at me. My finding the lost plane in an hour and a half when hundreds of planes had searched in vain for nearly a week was more than Joe could believe. Finally I turned away from Joe, went straight for a telephone and did what I should have done in the first place. I called the CAP (Civil Air Patrol) in Salt Lake City. When they answered, I asked if there had been any word on the Dykeses' plane. They said there was no chance of their being alive now and that the search had ended.

"Well, I've found them," I said. "And they're both alive."

Behind me, Joe stopped chewing me out, his eyes wide and his mouth open.

"I'll round up food and supplies," I continued to the CAP, "and the people here will get it to them as soon as possible." The CAP gave me the go-ahead.

Everyone at the airport went into action. Within one hour we were on our way. A local expert pilot, Hal Crumbo, would fly in the supplies. I would lead the way in another plane. I wasn't grounded for long!

Back in the air, we headed for the high peaks. Hal's plane was bigger and faster than the Aeronca I was in. He was flying out ahead and above me. When I got to Painters Basin, at eleven thousand feet, I met the severe downdrafts again. I could see Hal circling above me and knew he was in sight of the downed plane and ready to drop supplies. Since I couldn't go any higher, I turned around.

Back at the airport I joined a three-man ground rescue party, which would attempt to reach the couple on horseback.

Another rescue party had already left from the Wyoming side of the mountains. For the next twenty-four hours our party hiked through fierce winds and six-foot snowdrifts. At twelve thousand feet, on a ridge near Gilbert Peak, we stopped. In the distance, someone was yelling. Urging our freezing feet forward, we pressed on, tremendously excited. Suddenly, about a hundred yards in front of us, we saw the fuselage of a small red plane rammed into a snowbank. Nearby, two people flapped their arms wildly.

Charging ahead, we shouted with joy. At about the same time that we reached the Dykeses, the other rescue party was coming over the opposite ridge.

After much hugging and thanking, I learned what a miracle the Dykeses' survival was. They had had nothing to eat but a candy bar, and their clothing was scant—Mrs. Dykes had a fur coat, but her husband had only a topcoat. The altitude made starting a fire impossible and at night they huddled together in their downed plane, too afraid to go to sleep.

"We had all but given up, had even written notes as to who should look after the children," Mrs. Dykes said. Then turning to me, she said, "But when we saw your plane, it was the most wonderful thing . . . our prayers were answered, a dream come true."

"Yes," I said, smiling, suddenly feeling as Solomon in the Bible must have felt after he received a visit from the Lord one night in a dream (1 Kings 3:5–14).

My dream, like Solomon's, had occurred for a reason. In His own special way, God gave me that dream in order to help give life to two others. In the most mysterious of ways, He had shown me He is always there, always listening. He had heard my prayers and the Dykeses' prayers and had answered all of us in His own infallible way.

—*George Hunt*

The Cross That Wasn't There

For many years I operated a Christian bookstore beside our home north of Toronto, and on our lawn a large neon sign called to travelers on the busy highway that passes our house. We were accustomed to strangers dropping in.

But one July evening a man drove in and called my husband over to his car. He thrust the car keys into my husband's hands, saying, "Here, take these. I'm not fit to be on the road." He confessed that he'd had several drinks.

After talking for an hour, the man said, "I need help." My husband called up an organization that helps alcoholics, and two men from a nearby chapter came by. Later, having returned from work, I made a pot of coffee, and we sat around the kitchen table, talking.

He'd been on business at the beach thirty miles to our north. He was headed home, sixty-five miles to the south of us. "I could have killed someone," he repeated over and over. I thanked God that he had reached our house safely.

In the course of conversation I asked the man if he was familiar with this area.

"No," he said.

"Do you travel this way much?"

"No."

I was perplexed. "Why did you stop at our house?"

"The sign," he said. "I saw the sign on your lawn."

The sign? How could he have seen the sign? I had given it away when I closed the bookstore . . . nearly three years before. It was gone. There was nothing left of the yellow neon cross that once stood on our lawn.

Or was there?

—*Lois Taylor*

The Cross in the Water

One cold early evening many years ago, my wife, Bartie, and I set out in our cabin cruiser for a picnic dinner on south San

Francisco Bay. We waved to a college crew team heading out
for a practice row, then proceeded down the channel toward
the San Mateo Bridge. The choppy water soon turned into
huge waves.

At the drawbridge, I signaled to the bridge tender to let us
through. He shook his head, pointing to the whitecaps on the
water ahead. We were about to take our pitching craft home,
when in the distance near some mud flats, we saw a ruby-
colored light glowing, shimmering in the shape of a cross.
Bartie and I were mesmerized. We turned our craft in its
direction. It was irresponsible of me—in shallow muddy water
an engine might suck up mud that can destroy it—but I felt
compelled to follow the cross. Now mud was coming from the
exhaust pipe, and the temperature of our engine had risen into
the danger zone, but the light drew me on.

Then we came up to it, only to find that the light was merely
a buoy reflecting the red sunset. Bartie and I felt foolish; we
had actually risked our boat to chase a mirage.

"Look, the water is full of coconuts," Bartie said. But they
weren't coconuts at all; they were the men from the rowing
crew, whose shell had crashed into the bridge and sunk. One
by one we pulled them aboard. They had been in the water
for over an hour. Facing death, gulping the icy salt water, they
had come to a point of desperation and had prayed together
for rescue.

And that was when the cross began to shine for me.

—*Eros M. Savage*

My Sailor Boy

I was married at seventeen, and my children—one boy and
four girls—were born close together. The doctor said if I had
another baby, I would die. But before long I was expecting
again. The doctor said the pregnancy must be terminated. I
pondered and prayed. Reluctantly, I decided to comply, and
wearied from this decision, I lay down to rest.

After a brief nap I awoke to see—as clearly as I've ever seen anyone—a sailor boy. He was smiling and his sailor cap rested jauntily on the back of his head. On his forehead were short, shiny curls. I don't know why, but as I looked at this apparition, it came to me that I must cancel the impending surgery. I went on to bear a son named Robert.

Years later, in World War II, we received word that our elder son, Jack, had been killed. One day as I sat crying, young Robert touched my arm and said, "Mama, look at me. You've still got *me.*" With that intense statement from the heart of my little boy, my numbness began to recede.

Robert grew and then he, too, joined the service. He was stationed in Pearl Harbor and we didn't see him for a long time. Then we got a wire that he was coming home. The day before he was to arrive, I was in the kitchen mixing a cake when I heard the door open. I turned around, and standing there was the same sailor boy I'd seen years before. He was smiling and his sailor cap rested jauntily on the back of his head. On his forehead were short, shiny curls.

It took a moment for me to realize that this was my son Robert, surprising us by coming home a day early. It was Robert, the son I almost didn't have.

—*Ada Adams*
as told to *Phyllis Sjoblom*

The Picture in Aunt Lana's Mind

Pacific Beach, Washington, where Grandma and Aunt Lana lived for many years, is a very small town in a very bleak part of the world. Forlorn, one could call it. Not many people want to live there, or go there, for it rains incessantly, the people are poor, and the Pacific's waves are much too rough for surfing or swimming. Still, I loved my visits there, and never more than during the summer of 1973, when Aunt Lana included me in one of her spiritual "adventures." It was an adventure in blind trust.

Aunt Lana and Grandma went to live in Pacific Beach because that's the only place where Aunt Lana could find employment. She's a teacher. She is also handicapped. In 1949, she was struck down by polio, and this robust, six-foot-two woman has been in a wheelchair ever since. Aunt Lana is a triumphant woman, however, with a hard, practical hold on life and a bold grip on the life of the spirit. I think she's especially attuned to spiritual things *because* she's handicapped and not running around wastefully the way most of us are.

On the last day of my summer visit in 1973, when I was fourteen, I realized that something was troubling Aunt Lana. The sun was dancing across the surf when I went down to the kitchen that lovely morning. But as we breakfasted on apricots, toast and hard-boiled eggs, Aunt Lana was silent. Not so Grandma. "The sun always shines over a day in Pacific Beach," she said cheerily. "But for the rest of the day you'd better keep your coat on."

We cleared the table, and just as I was about to go back upstairs, I saw Aunt Lana sitting in her room, just staring.

"Anything I can do?" I said, concerned. She shook her head. Then as I was about to leave, she changed her mind.

"Well, maybe there *is* something you can do. I'm stymied."

She told me a strange story about a picture that had come into her mind a few days before. She hadn't paid much attention to it at first, for it was simply a scene that had flashed into her consciousness—some sand and some rocks and a body of water, that's all. But the scene kept coming back, persistently intruding on her prayers and thoughts.

"I have a feeling that the picture comes from the Lord, that He's trying to tell me something," Aunt Lana said. "But what?"

To me, this was pretty deep spiritual stuff. I felt a little timid about presuming to advise Aunt Lana in this special area of hers, but I was soon deeply involved—and fascinated. We talked for a while, and then, remembering that Aunt Lana loved stories, I said, "What do you think one of your detectives would do?" That started Aunt Lana taking the picture apart piece by piece, as though each held a clue.

"All right," she said, closing her eyes and summoning the picture into view. "The sun is shining. There's water on the left, sand on the right, a bluff of rock hovering over that—so that must be north. And if that's so, then this is very likely a beach on the West Coast."

"Maybe one here in Washington?"

"Yes, it looks like our shoreline," Aunt Lana replied, "but there's nothing to distinguish it, no man-made thing." She was silent now, her eyes still closed. "But the water," she said so suddenly that I jumped, "look at the water! It's smooth, no ripples. That could mean a cove of some sort." Then a little sadly, "But not on this wild coast of ours."

Aunt Lana and I wrestled with these meager facts for a little while, and then we had to admit that we could make nothing of them. Still, Aunt Lana couldn't shake the conviction that the picture had some special meaning for her.

At noon we were just getting ready to dry the luncheon dishes and Aunt Lana was reaching for the dish towel when her hand stopped in mid-air. "Bobby," she said, "there's some quiet water up north of here, up in the Indian reservation. I feel sure I've seen some."

"Let's try to find it," I said, and with a flurry of excitement we made plans for the search. We were about ready to leave when Grandma suggested that as long as we were heading up near the Quinault reservation, we might drop off some old clothes she'd been saving to give away. Aunt Lana thought that a good idea. One of her students lived up in Taholah with an aged grandmother. Maybe they'd have some use for them.

With Aunt Lana at the wheel of her white Impala—with the hand brake she'd designed herself and had someone weld— we headed north. The road paralleled the ocean, winding over hills and through creek canyons. We passed storm-sculptured rocks where sea birds took shelter from the turbulent breakers. Bizarre pillars of stone dotted the beaches like human forms in windblown garments. "The Indians say that those pillars are women waiting for the men to return from the sea," Aunt Lana said, filling me with wonderful facts about the Quinault Indians who once had earned their livelihood from whaling.

We traveled on. The road narrowed and threatened to become gravel, though it never quite did. Soon we crossed into the Quinault reservation. About a mile or so deeper in, she stopped the car. "Point Grenville!" she shouted. "Quick,

Bob, over there! Run to the beach. See what's there." I was out of the car lickety-split, and in a few minutes came panting back.

"It's there!" I called. I described the cove with the ocean on the left and the beach with the looming rocks on the right, and the sun's rays glistening on the water's quiet ripples.

Aunt Lana threw up her arms in a wild expression of joy. She reached over and hugged me and kissed me on the fore-head. Then she became serious. "Now tell me what else you saw."

"I didn't see anything else, Aunt Lana."

"Nobody was there?"

"Nobody."

"You didn't see anything odd?" I shook my head. Aunt Lana's face darkened. She put her head down on the steering wheel; I knew she was praying.

"Well," she said finally, "I don't know what it means. Sty-mied again."

It seemed a shame to give up now. We discussed the possi-bility of our just staying there and waiting for something to happen, and for a while that's what we did. As time passed, I guess we both felt disillusioned. At one point I looked into the back seat and saw the boxes of clothes Grandma had given us; I suggested that we bring them to the Indian family.

"What clothes?" Aunt Lana said. She'd forgotten about them. My idea prevailed, however, and we started up again and drove toward the little town huddled in a small valley by a river. In Taholah, Aunt Lana drove up to the fish cannery and sent me in with instructions to buy a fish for dinner. I bought a small salmon, wrapped it in three layers of the *Aberdeen World,* and put it in the trunk. Fishing meant jobs, and the noble salmon provided for the needs of many of the town's families, most of whom were desperately poor.

After that we drove to Second Street and turned down it. The houses we passed were blank-walled—the Indians thought that a house facing the street would be haunted and bring bad luck. We drove to the house on the corner, the only one that was painted—a bright canary yellow with a blue stripe around the middle. Aunt Lana honked the horn and presently a small child toddled out, squinted at us, and ran back inside.

"The grandmother is very old," Aunt Lana explained to me. "I am told that she has eighteen children of her own, and who knows how many grandchildren."

Soon the old grandmother appeared. By the time she shuffled up to Aunt Lana's door, I was out of the car and waiting with a box of clothes. The old Indian reached out to touch Aunt Lana's outstretched hand. "You've come," she said. "I've been expecting you."

Aunt Lana and I looked at each other. Then we both looked at the grandmother. Perhaps we hadn't heard her correctly.

"You were expecting us?"

"Yes, yes," she said, and gradually, in stops and starts, fumbling for words, she told us about the trouble in the family, the people out of work, someone in jail, the hunger, the lack of warm clothing, the ever-pervasive need. Then one day, she continued, when her feeling of helplessness was at its worst, she had wandered down to the beach.

As the old woman mentioned the word "beach," I saw a glimmer come into Aunt Lana's eyes. "And then?" Aunt Lana said.

"I walk along the edge of the water. A long time." As she talked I pictured her moving aimlessly among the rocks while the great waves thundered and splashed. "Then I come to a place where the ocean is more quiet and the wind is very kind . . ."

A cove, I wanted to say. *You came to a cove.*

". . . and there I talk to God. 'Please, God,' I say, 'tell someone to bring help. Not for me, God—for the little ones.' "

It was almost unnecessary to ask her when she had prayed in the quiet cove. I knew, Aunt Lana knew, that the old woman had been talking to her God three days before, the very day, the very hour, when the picture first came into Aunt Lana's mind. And so it proved to be.

I carried the boxes of clothes into the house while Aunt Lana sat in the car making arrangements for help. Then we left. The old grandmother, surrounded now by a crowd of children, waved good-bye. "God is taking care," I heard her say. "God is taking care."

At the end of the day, just before leaving Aunt Lana's home

for my own, I took a last walk on the beach. I wore a coat to shield me from the windblown rain. The beginning of a storm from the southwest brought waves that washed my rubber boots. It had been a day like no others, a day in which Aunt Lana had helped me learn what she had known for a long time: that God has countless ways of letting us know that He is there, taking care.

—Robert J. Foss

It's More Than a Dream

I suppose none of us knows the meaning of dreams. But I know what prayers can do.

I was working the three-to-eleven shift at Miners Hospital in Spangler, Pennsylvania, when a patient I was feeding asked, "Why don't you have a little pin on like the other nurses?"

"I do," I said, reaching to show him the golden, wreath-shaped R.N. pin on my collar—one of my proudest possessions. It had been given to me when I graduated from nursing school in Altoona, and it stood for years of hard work and study. But now, when I looked down, the pin was gone.

I knew I had pinned it to my uniform just before I left the house. I looked everywhere for it. A colleague and I searched through all the linens and bedside equipment but found nothing. I even took a mop and dusted under the beds. At home I turned the place upside down. No pin. Of course, I could replace it, but a substitute would never mean as much. That night as I lay in bed, I prayed that the Lord would help me find it.

Soon I was asleep. In the deep of night I had a dream. I dreamed that I got out of bed, put on my duster and slippers, and ran downstairs and out the door to a puddle of water in front of the house. And in the puddle was my pin.

The next morning I awoke disappointed. "It was only a dream," I muttered to myself. "A worthless dream." But as my head cleared, I seemed to hear a voice saying, *No, it's more than a dream. Go. See.*

I put on my duster and slippers and walked out to the road in front of our house, and there found a puddle of water. I placed my hand into the brown water. In a moment I held in my hand an answered prayer.

—*Mary LaMagna Rocco*

A Calendar for Courage

The gatekeeper at our mission compound limped into the kitchen doorway, bowed crookedly, and announced, *"Hsieh si-mu,* pastor's wife, here is his excellency, the colonel."

I held my breath. The colonel commanded the troops currently protecting this city of Shenkiu in Central China. It was January 1941; the invading Japanese were only a few miles to the east.

The colonel entered briskly and made his announcement: "The enemy is advancing into Honan Province. We have orders not to defend this city. You should find refuge in one of the villages outside."

I crossed my hands over the sleeves of my wadded *e-shang* and bowed politely, thanking him for his gracious concern for a "miserable" woman. As the colonel left the room, the icy January blast swept through the doorway. My baby cried. Suddenly the enormity of our danger overwhelmed me.

Our Margaret Anne was scarcely two months old, Johnny just over a year. Yesterday my husband, urgently needing medical care, had been taken by rickshaw to the hospital 115 miles away. I looked at the little Daily Scripture calendar on the wall: January 15. Not until early February would he be back. How would I manage without him? How would I make the myriad decisions that now crowded upon me?

You see, I had not yet experienced the full wonder of God's power to guide us when all other guides fail.

Nor did I guess that as His instrument He would use anything as prosaic as a calendar on a kitchen wall.

By mid-afternoon the army garrison in our little city was empty. The departure of the soldiers created panic. Families packed their goods and fled.

The elders of the church called on me before they left. "Come with us," they pleaded. "We will care for you while Pastor Hillis is away."

I looked at the concern in their eyes and I thought of the country homes to which they were headed. My husband and I loved these village homes because we loved the people in them. But they held death for Western babies, as too many little graves in our mission compounds showed.

How could I explain to these friends—without offending—that I could not take my children into their homes? Unheated, mud-floored huts, they crowded three and four generations together amid vermin and filth. Just a few weeks ago the six-month-old son of the nearest American family had died of dreaded dysentery. No, my babies were chained to this kitchen where I could boil dishes, milk and water.

But these were not things I could say to Chinese friends. I bowed, I thanked them, I spoke of waiting for my husband's return, of watching the mission property—and I went to bed that night shaking with terror. When Johnny woke up whimpering in the cold, I took him into bed with me and lay awake a long time, listening to the wind rattle the waxed paper windowpanes and praying that my little boy would live to see his daddy again.

Next morning I was in the kitchen early to start the water boiling for Margaret Anne's bottle. Automatically I reached up to the wall calendar and tore off yesterday's date. The Scripture verse for the new day gleamed like sunlight. "What time I am afraid, I will trust in thee" (Psalm 56:3).

Well, I was certainly afraid. I fulfilled that part of it. Now, indeed, was the time to trust God. Somehow the verse sustained me all through the tense day.

The city was being evacuated rapidly. Other church members came to invite me to their family huts. But the Scripture held me. I was *not* to panic, but to *trust.*

By mid-morning the next day the city was nearly deserted. Then the gatekeeper came to me, eyes blurred with fear. He must leave, he said, and begged me to find refuge with him in his village beyond the city.

Should I? What could I do without our gatekeeper? The deserted city would be an open invitation to bandits and loot-

ers. But the risk to my babies outside was certain; here I
still faced only fears. I declined the gatekeeper's offer,
and watched him as he sorrowfully took leave.

It was noon before I remembered to pull the page off the
little daily calendar on the wall. The tenth verse of the ninth
Psalm read, "And they that know thy name will put their trust
in thee: for thou, Lord, hast not forsaken them that seek thee."

As I bowed my head over my noonday meal, my heart
poured out its gratitude to God for these particular words at
this moment.

My main concern now was food. All the shops in the town
were boarded shut. Meat and produce no longer came in daily
from farms. I still had the goats for the babies' milk, but the
man who milked them had left for his village. Tomorrow I
would have to try to milk them myself. I wondered if I could
ever make the balky little beasts hold still.

I slept uneasily that night, wondering how I would feed my
children, and sure of very little except that we should stay in
the city and, somehow, trust God. The sound of distant gunfire
woke me.

Before facing the goats, I fixed myself a bowl of rice gruel.
Then I tore the old page from the calendar and read the new
day's message. "I will nourish you, and your little ones," said
the God of promise (Genesis 50:21).

The timeliness of these daily verses was becoming almost
uncanny. With some curiosity I examined the back of the
calendar pad. It had been put together in England the year
before, but God in His all-knowing had provided the very
words I needed, a year later, here on the other side of the
world.

I was still eating the gruel when a woman stepped into the
kitchen. She was carrying a pail of steaming goats' milk. "May
I stay and help you?" she asked. "See, I have milked your
goats."

Mrs. Lee had been our neighbor for years, but that morning
I stared at her as though she had dropped from heaven. She
had no family living, she explained, and wished to show her
gratitude to the mission.

Late in the day a loud rapping at the gate set our hearts

pounding. Braver, Mrs. Lee was the one who went to open it. Her face beaming, she returned leading our caller.

"Gee-tze! Gee-dan!" she cried triumphantly. "Chicken! Eggs!"

A frail, black-robed country woman came in with a live chicken and a basket of eggs. "Peace, peace," she gave the customary Christian greeting as she bobbed to us shyly. Noise of the cannons had not kept her away when she remembered that the missionaries would be hungry.

The calendar promise had come true! God *would* see to it that our little ones were nourished! That night my heart was full of hope. To the sound of shells bursting in the sky I prayed that somehow God would spare this city and these gentle people whom we loved.

Next morning I rushed down to the little square of paper hanging on its nail and tore off the page. "When I cry unto thee, then shall mine enemies turn back: this I know; for God is for me," the Scripture declared (Psalm 56:9).

But this time it was too much to believe! Surely it couldn't be right to take literally a verse chosen just by chance for an English calendar?

As the gunfire drew closer, Mrs. Lee and I began to prepare the house for invasion. Any papers that might possibly be construed to have military or political significance must be hidden or destroyed. We searched my husband's desk and the church buildings. By nightfall the gunfire sounded from both sides of the city. We went to bed dressed, prepared at any moment to meet the Japanese invaders.

I awoke abruptly in the early dawn and strained my ears for the crunch of military boots on gravel. But only a deep stillness surrounded me. There were no tramping feet, no shrieking shells or pounding guns, only the waking murmur of little Johnny in his crib.

Misgivings warred with excitement as I woke Mrs. Lee and we went to the gatehouse, each carrying a child. She was the first to stick out a cautious head. "There is no one in the street," she told me. "Shall we go out?"

And then, we stepped through the gate and watched as the streets began to fill, not with Japanese soldiers, but with townspeople returning from their country hiding places. Had the Chinese won?

As if in answer to our question, we met the colonel. "Pastor's wife!" he greeted me with relief. "I have been concerned about you!"

Then he told us that the Japanese had withdrawn. No, they had not been defeated, nor could anyone arrive at a reasonable conjecture concerning their retreat. The enemy had simply turned back.

I stepped into my kitchen, eyes fixed on a little block of paper pinned to the wall. Oh, you could say it was just a calendar. You could say strangers had chosen those verses without any thought of China, or of the war that would be raging when those dates fell due. But to me it was more than a calendar, and no stranger had picked those lines. To me it was the handwriting of God.

—*Margaret Hillis*

GOD
RESCUES

*I waited patiently for the Lord; and he . . .
heard my cry. He brought me up also out of an
horrible pit, out of the miry clay, and set my
feet upon a rock, and established my goings.*
                            —Psalm 40:1–2

There are times when life brings trouble and danger that we cannot avoid. But there is also trouble we get into because we don't hear God speaking—because we haven't taken time to listen or haven't learned to recognize His voice in our peaceful hours. Yet these stories show us that even in those times God still reaches out to show us His love.

God uses many means to take us out of danger. Unexpected and unexplained people may appear out of nowhere to help us—the Bible describes such people as "angels of the Lord."

Sometimes He helps us see that we already have the means to rescue ourselves—a pencil, some fried chicken, a canned ham. God's part is to call our attention to what is already in our hand. Our part is to use it.

Sometimes He brings about the rescue by letting rescuers know in strange ways what to do, where to go—or just that they are needed. Screams, both uttered and unuttered, a burned-out radio—God can use anything.

At other times rescue comes through actions that are physically impossible—like tractors rolling uphill by themselves, or a runaway bus coming to a complete stop going downhill.

The greatest story of rescue is given to us in the Bible, the Book of Exodus, when God brought a whole nation—the people of Israel—out of slavery in Egypt. He shut them up in an impossible situation between mountains, sea, and an army—and then miraculously opened up a way through the sea, closing it after they were all through safely.

The Bible also tells of a different kind of rescue—one with long-reaching consequences. The young Joseph was threatened with death by his brothers. But his first rescue only worsened his situation because he was sold into slavery. Eventually, because of a series of dreams, he was "rescued" from prison and brought into the position to save his world from starvation. This is a story to remember when we don't see anything changing in our difficulties, or when we perhaps even see things getting worse. God is still with us, and means only good for us.

The Cloud

Twice in my life I have seen and felt a phenomenon so strange to me, so irrational, that it took an act of faith to believe it. Twice, each time during a period of grave trouble, a thing that looked like a cloud, a misty white cloud, has come to me. Once it helped save my life. Bizarre? Of course. The only thing I have ever been able to liken it to are the clouds mentioned in the Bible, especially that helpful cloud described in the Book of Exodus and in the letters of Saint Paul.

My first encounter with this cloud was many years ago in Detroit. I was seven months pregnant when a doctor told me that I had diabetes. This was shattering news, not just because of the coming baby, but because my father had suffered from the same disease and I knew all about the needles and the diet and the strain.

On the way home that day I saw an announcement for an evangelist then conducting healing services at the Detroit Fair Grounds. Ordinarily this would have meant nothing to me. I was not a very spiritually oriented person. Growing up I'd passed through a variety of Sunday schools, but I was not a churchgoer. I believed in a Supreme Being, and from time to time I prayed—that was about the sum of my religion. Nevertheless, one evening I went alone, secretly, and stood in the back of the evangelist's tent. I prayed earnestly. Nothing happened. Still, I went on praying for several days. And that's what I was doing as I stood at the kitchen stove preparing dinner late one afternoon when I looked up and there, hovering above me, was the cloud. At first I thought it was some peculiar accumulation of steam from the stove, but it didn't dissolve; it held its shape, a cottony mass about two feet long. I could have reached up and touched it, but I was afraid to.

Then it moved. Slowly it began to roll, to swirl. To my utter astonishment, this swirling mist descended on me and disappeared into my body. It just faded into me. I could feel it vibrating within me.

I was too startled, too mystified, to tell anybody about it. In fact, I mentioned it to no one until a few days later when a woman appeared at my door in response to a card I must have filled out at the tent. Soon I found myself describing the cloud to her. She nodded. "It was the healing virtue," she said.

I did not know what that meant, and so my visitor explained about the ailing woman who touched Christ's garment and was healed. Together we read the passage from Mark: "And straightway the fountain of her blood was dried up; and she felt in her body that she was healed of that plague. And Jesus, immediately knowing in himself that virtue had gone out of him . . ." (Mark 5:29–30).

For a while I was hopeful that this astonishing experience meant that I had been healed, but that was not so. The diabetes has remained with me from that day to this, though it has always puzzled doctors that my condition has never deteriorated. Since I was not cured, however, I pushed the experience with the white cloud into a recess of my memory, and the years passed.

On November 17, 1974, my husband and I were cruising along in our custom-built motor home, heading west on Highway I-10, hugging the Texas side of the Rio Grande. Scotty had recently retired as an executive of the Ford Motor Company in Dearborn, Michigan, and now we were on our way to our winter home in Arizona.

Near sundown, we pulled into a large, paved roadside park. It was surrounded by desert, nothing but scrubby chaparral in sight. There were several cars in the parking area when we arrived. Gradually these left until only one remained, a yellow-and-black sports car.

I set the table for dinner while Scotty walked our four-year-old schnauzer, Fritz. When they returned and I opened the door for them, what I saw made me gasp. Coming up behind Scotty was a young man with a pistol in his hand.

"What's wrong?" Scotty said to me, and then the gun touched his back.

"Get in!" the young man ordered. With a rough shove he pushed Scotty inside. The gunman was about twenty years old, short-haired, clean-shaven, neatly dressed in brown slacks and a brown turtleneck sweater. His face was grim, his voice expressionless.

"All right, get your cash." Scotty reached for his wallet, took out the money in it. The gunman stuffed it in his pocket.

"Now you."

My purse was on the bed, yet I was so afraid I couldn't move. He snapped, "Move, lady!" I got my purse, reached in and removed three bills.

"Okay, now, a buddy of mine is out there in the bushes. He's got something he wants to talk over with you." He waved the pistol toward the door, but we hesitated. If we stalled for time, somebody might drive in.

"I've made some wonderful chili," I said, grabbing at straws. "Have some with us." He put the gun to my head. "Get moving."

At that moment I figured he was going to steal our motor home, and if he did he might take Fritz along with it. "May I please take my little dog?" I asked.

"I won't hurt him, lady," was all he said as he forced us out into the desert. With the sun down now, it was cold. We came to a barbed wire fence. There were five strands of wire, each spaced a foot apart. The gunman held the bottom wire while I crawled under. This unexpected act of courtesy on his part inspired me to try another tack with him.

"You must have been awfully abused as a little boy to come to this . . ."

"Shut up. Don't get smart," he snapped at me, but I could see now that he, too, was trembling. A new fear came into my mind: He might shoot us accidentally.

"Help me, Jesus," I cried under my breath. "Help me, Lord," I prayed.

A hundred, two hundred yards we walked. "That's far enough. Turn around. My buddy's behind that bush."

As I turned, I saw no one behind the creosote bush he pointed toward. "Take off your clothes."

"Please," Scotty pleaded, "don't do any—"

"Strip," he said, "both of you."

As we stripped down to our underwear, he made us place our clothing into two piles. "Lay face down on your clothes," came the command.

I thought he was going to tie us up until I looked over and saw Scotty staring up at the gun. "My God!" Scotty shouted, horrified. "You're not going to—"

But the young man began firing, first at Scotty, then at me.

Something rose up and out from within me. A cloud. The misty white cloud I had seen all those years before hovered over me once more like one of those comic strip balloons.

I found myself floating in the air in spirit form. I could look down and see my own body on the ground below, beside Scotty's. I felt at peace. Comfortable. No pain. But this lasted only briefly.

The next thing I remember I was standing up, staggering somewhere, I did not know where, in my bare feet. Blood flowed over my eyes. I bumped into something. A creosote bush. Swaying, I held on to one of its prickly offshoots. "Help me, Jesus, help me. Lord God, help me," I prayed.

The cloud appeared again, larger this time. I accepted its being there without amazement. "Move to the left," a voice said. I moved to the left. The cloud moved, wrapped itself about my body, buoyed my arms, supported me. "See the lights?" asked the voice. I squinted, my eyes barely open. Yes. Now I remembered, the lights of the roadside park. With the cloud holding me, I groped forward, then stopped. "See the post?" There was the post of the barbed wire fence. I went to it and clung to it. The cloud went away.

I stood there weakly holding on, trying to focus my mind. If only I could make it to the parking area, I could lie there until somebody drove in. If I collapsed here, I'd die unnoticed.

The very next thing I knew, I was on the other side of the fence.

I could not comprehend how I had got there. Nor did I try, for it was my feet that troubled me now. They were a mass of thorns and sandburs. Walking on them was torture. I summoned up my energy. I propelled myself, half walking, half crawling, to the pavement of the parking area. The motor home was gone. I stumbled down at last, my head on the cold surface of a picnic table. In spite of the horror, in spite of the pain, I was calm. "Thank You, Lord, thank You," I kept saying out loud with every gasp of breath.

"Chloe, Chloe," came my name, called in a faint voice. Scotty's voice. I looked up and there was Scotty, standing dazedly in the middle of the park pavement, coughing now as though the words he had spoken were strangling him.

I spoke to him matter-of-factly. "I've over here, Scotty." He came and slumped down beside me. We were too dazed from the bullets to do anything but silently recognize each other's existence.

I raised my head. A car was coming. Now it was coming into the park area.

"Help, help," we both said, more moaning than shouting. We got to our feet, our arms flailing above us as the lights of the car spotlighted us. But the car swerved and sped out onto the highway again. I collapsed.

The minutes passed. I could hear another car coming. Then more cars, sirens. I heard the sound of running footsteps. I felt the warmth of a blanket. I felt strong arms holding me.

Much later, safely out of cranial surgery and days of intensive care (though both our skulls were battered, neither of us had any brain damage, any paralysis, or even a concussion), Scotty and I learned of our rescue by a young man named Tommy Rodriguez who had just driven away from having coffee with the sheriff at a nearby diner. Spotting us, and not wanting the sheriff to get away, Tommy had made a fast turn-around—only seemingly deserting us—and sped away.

Once the police arrived, I passed out intermittently, but Scotty remained coherent enough to tell his name, age, the make of our motor home, its license number! His years as an automotive executive did not fail him as he told the police about the "two-toned yellow-and-black Dodge Charger with Utah plates on it"—enough information for a radio call that enabled the police fifteen miles away to pick up the sports car, the motor home (with our little Fritz, safe and sound in it), the young man who shot us, as well as his accomplice. Eventually, these two were tried and sent to prison.

After seventeen days in the Eastwood Hospital in El Paso, we were taken back to the roadside park. I wanted to see the scene again, to check a point in my own mind.

It was all there as I remembered it: the spot where I'd looked down upon our two bodies, the creosote bush I had held on to, the post I had clung to, the stains on it still visible. And there was the barbed wire fence. To me, that was the real key to the reality of my cloud. It simply wasn't possible that, in my blinded, stumbling condition, I could have crawled through those five closely spaced strands of barbed wire unassisted—without being scratched. Yet, among all my wounds, there were no scratches on my body, or on Scotty's. Now I was certain. Something had helped me through—or over—the barbed wire.

Twice since that terrible experience I have read The Living Bible through from beginning to end, and many times I have returned to the same passage in much the same way one seeks out an old and dear friend: "For we must never forget, dear brothers, what happened to our people in the wilderness long ago. God guided them by sending a cloud that moved along ahead of them; and he brought them all safely through the waters of the Red Sea. This might be called their 'baptism'— baptized both in sea and cloud!" (1 Corinthians 10:1–2).

Looking back today, I know that that night of terror was not without its blessings. Never again will death frighten me. If it was so that I was dead and my spirit rose above my body, I found the sensation sweet and placid and natural. On the other hand, never will life frighten me either. I savor it. I believe that the cloud that came to me twice dwells within me today. It stirs; I feel loved and wanted. It heals. It comforts. Call it what you will, I believe it is the Holy Spirit of Jesus.

—*Chloe Wardrop*

The Silent Screams—I

The Chicago neighborhood I grew up in was a friendly place, but ever since I was a little girl my mother had warned me not to accept rides from strangers. Still, one frigid day when a man in a truck offered a lift, I climbed aboard.

I knew the moment the door slammed shut that I was in trouble. It was something about the way he looked at me. "You passed the grocery," I said meekly. "Please stop." He said nothing. "I want to get out," I said.

"Don't touch that door!" he ordered. The truck speeded up. From his coat he drew forth a knife and skimmed it along my leg. "Any noise out of you," he warned, "any noise at all and . . ." He made a violent dagger gesture.

I could hear myself screaming inside, but no sounds were

coming out of my mouth. *Our Father, Who art in Heaven
. . .* I began silently saying the Lord's Prayer . . . *hallowed be
Thy name . . .*

The truck turned into an alley and stopped. I fumbled for
the door handle. The man reached over and pushed the door
open so swiftly that I fell out. I tried to get up to run, but he
was there standing over me, and I saw the knife again. *Thy will
be done . . .*

Down the alley I heard running steps and wild yelling. The
man leaped up. A policeman jumped on him as a woman
picked me up. "Are you all right?" she kept saying to me. And
then, "Thank God that I heard your screams."

But no sound had come from my mouth. Except in my head,
there had been no screams.

—Ellen Daveys

The Silent Screams—II

It was near dusk when I heard that unearthly scream from the
woods nearby where I was working. I don't spook easily, but
I could feel a cold ripple of fear.

I'd come alone from town to our isolated farm to tinker with
some tractors. "I'll probably stay overnight," I'd told my wife,
Doris.

Now, as I picked up my wrench, the weird cry came a
second time—not human, not animal. And it was louder,
closer.

That did it. I *had* to get out of there. I jumped into my truck
and barreled down the lonely back road toward home. Then,
rounding a curve, I came upon a scene as startling as the
scream that still echoed in my head. A truck was carelessly
parked at the side of the road—the door open, motor idling,
lights on. Beside it lay the body of a man.

I braked hard and pulled in behind the truck. *He's had a heart
attack,* I thought to myself. But bending over the unconscious
figure—he was in his twenties—I could see blood pulsing from
a wound in his left thigh.

I don't have any medical training, but I knew this boy was bleeding to death. I tore off my belt. As I cinched it tight around his leg like a tourniquet, another car stopped and the driver hurried up to me. "Help me get him in my truck," I told him. "Call the rescue squad, and I'll drive ahead to meet them."

Later, we learned that Jeffrey Brumfield's rifle had jolted off the seat and fired into his leg, piercing a major artery. Doctors barely managed to save his life—and shattered leg.

Jeffrey might well have died, they said. But I had heard an eerie scream—eight miles away from a victim who had blacked out.

—*Royal Krantz*

SOS

Vietnam, December 14, 1967—just before the first Tet Offensive. I was with Charlie Company, First Battalion, 25th Lightning Division, near Saigon. In the afternoon a Vietcong death squad hit us, leaving ten dead. At sundown, feeling jittery, I went on patrol. Gribbit, Vigor and I set up a listening post about five hundred meters from camp. At 1:00 A.M., I reported in: "This is Charlie, L.P. One. Lots of movement out here."

The radio on my back crackled: "Get down . . . we're going to fire." Our guys started throwing rockets into the bush; the enemy started their own barrage. We were pinned down. "O God! Get us *out* of here . . . please!" I prayed as I chewed dirt.

There was a thud, like someone punching my back. A grenade exploded. I felt blood trickling down my back. "We've been hit," I radioed, "we're coming in!" In spite of our wounds, we scrambled in the darkness through a field of claymore mines and bales of razor-sharp wire and stumbled into the arms of the arriving medics.

Three weeks later, when all three of us were out of the hospital and back at camp, my platoon sergeant called me in. "Coverdale, how did you guys manage to let the medics know you'd been hit?"

"Radio, sir." I was surprised he should ask.

"Not with *this,* soldier," he replied, holding up a twisted, blackened box. It was the radio I had carried on my back. It had taken the full blast of the grenade, probably saving my life. And in doing so, the batteries, the crystal—every component—had been destroyed.

How did the medics get my SOS? I don't know. But God does.

—*Thomas Coverdale*

"I Heard Her Yell in English"

That hot summer Illinois afternoon my wife and I had been invited to a swimming party at the home of some friends.

With our two children in the care of my grandmother, Cherie and I felt as free as the breeze. As I stood on the diving board, I paused to look up into the serene sky.

But then a frantic voice rose above the party din. At the far end of the pool a woman was screaming. "The baby!" I heard her cry. "He's at the bottom of the pool!"

But no one was doing anything to help. People just stood and stared at her. Confused, I searched the length of the pool and saw what I thought might be a motionless form beneath the water. I dived in—and a baby *was* there. I hurriedly swept him off the bottom and soon laid him on the deck. He'd turned blue . . . no breath. I began CPR.

"Dear God. Help me do it right."

At last the little boy coughed. A short breath came, then another. He would live.

An ambulance was called, for safety's sake. While we waited, I couldn't help asking the others, "Why did you ignore the woman when she said the boy was drowning?"

A friend answered, "None of us understood her, Scott."

"What do you mean? Even at the far end I could hear her yelling about the baby."

"But she's Mexican. None of us understood her Spanish."

"Spanish? I heard her yell in English."

"We didn't. All we heard was Spanish."

"It's true," said the woman's daughter. "Mama can't speak a word of English."

To this day I'm still bewildered. I don't understand a word of Spanish.

—*Scott Brostrom*

The Earthmover

"Child choking! . . . Handle Code Three!" Dreaded words. I responded immediately, flipping on red lights and siren as the dispatcher gave the address and directions. *Just my luck,* I thought as I sped past parked cars, and passed drivers who did not pull over on the highway.

I had just begun my working day. Actually it was my day off, and I had been called in to cover for another officer who was ill. I knew next to nothing about this particular beat in Los Angeles and intended to drive around it to familiarize myself with the area. Now, my first call was a life-and-death emergency several miles away.

I had been a patrol officer for some time, but no matter how many life-and-death situations an officer faces, when a child is involved the heart beats a little faster, the foot is a little heavier on the accelerator, the urgency is greater.

I decided to take the unfinished freeway; it was next to impossible to get through the traffic on Highway 101. Just ahead was the street that would take me to my destination. Then, anguish swept through me. *There was no off-ramp.* Between me and that road was a deep, wide ditch and a steep embankment.

Tires screeched as I stopped, red lights still flashing. I got out and looked down at the busy road so far below me.

God help me! I cried out silently. *What am I going to do? If I go around I'll be too late.*

"What's the matter, Officer?"

I looked up, and saw a man sitting on top of the biggest

earth-moving vehicle I have ever seen. He must have been
sitting two stories high.

"Child choking to death . . . I have to get down there,"
I gestured blindly, "but there's no road. If I go around I'll
never make it."

Years of discipline had taught me to control my emotions,
but I was in an agony of frustration.

"Follow me, Officer—*I'll make you a road!*"

I jumped in my car and took off after him, amazed at what
the mammoth machine could do. The huge buckets on the side
of it were full of dirt. He dumped them into the ditch.

The clock had become my enemy.

Hurry! Hurry! Hurry!

The earthmover started down the long sloping embankment, scattering dirt. Huge clouds of dust enveloped us. It
seemed like hours, but in reality it was a short time before the
earthmover lumbered down on the highway, blocking traffic
in both directions.

Hurry!

I raced, siren screaming, the few short blocks to the street
I had been given, and frantically searched for the correct address. Almost at once I found it.

As I burst through the doorway, a terrified young mother
handed me her tiny baby boy. I could see she was going to be
no help. The baby was already blue. Was I too late?

"God . . . help."

All I remember about the next few seconds was turning the
baby upside down, smacking his back. The deadly object flew
from his throat onto the floor. It was a button that had let a
tiny bit of air through, but not enough.

I was aware of another siren.

A fireman rushed into the room.

Precious oxygen.

The child screamed, turned red, flailing his tiny fists. He was
angry, but very much alive.

Back in my car I logged the incident, reported in by radio,
and drove down the street, shaken, but elated.

I glanced up at the sky. "Thank You."

This, then, was what it was all about. Lately I had found

myself wondering if this kind of life was really worthwhile. The hostile, the criminals, the dregs of society. The petty little things that took time and energy to deal with. A thankless job. Was this the life I wanted?

Yet, with God's help, we had just saved a baby's life. And, in this act, my own life had suddenly come into perspective. That little mite in distress had taught me that I had important work to do and that I would be helped in this work by a loving, caring God who would hear a prayer and help a troubled cop get his car over a ditch.

Another call came. Then another, and so on through the day.

The next day I was determined to learn the patrol area before anything else happened. I never wanted to get caught like that again. As I drove along I approached the place where I had stood in desperation twenty-four hours before. I slowed as I again saw the gigantic earthmover. I wanted to thank him. The driver waved and yelled.

As he ran toward me, I could see he was deeply moved. He stammered, "The . . . the baby . . ." He stopped, unable to speak.

Surprised at his deep emotion, I tried to reassure him, "The baby is all right. Thanks to you—you helped save his life. I never would have made it in time. Man, that was teamwork."

He gulped, "I . . . I know . . . but what I didn't know when . . . when I helped you was . . ." He bit his lip hard, then added in a whisper, "That was my son."

—Les Brown

Flash Flood

It had been an unusually wet June. The morning of the sixteenth it was drizzling, but the weatherman had predicted just showers, so we had no reason to expect anything more than an ordinary rainy day.

My husband, Reuben, and I were driving from Denver to our home in Castle Rock, Colorado. We were still a bit somber and saddened for we had gone to Denver for my brother's funeral. Increasingly heavy rain seemed to darken our spirits even more.

As we were driving south on Highway 85, visibility became poor and the steady accumulation of water on the road made for slow driving. Soon we realized this was not an ordinary rainstorm. A fierce wind—now seeming to have almost the intensity of a tornado—began pushing our car back and forth along the highway.

I gripped the car door as rocks washed onto the road, making things even more treacherous. It was taking all of Reuben's skill as a driver to keep from hitting the rocks, some of which were as large as washtubs.

As we crept along, the water rose and soon was up to our hubcaps. Ahead of us, cars began sliding off the road one by one, ending up stuck in the sand on the road shoulder. Afraid of stalling, we kept going. Suddenly a huge wall of water came crashing down upon us from the hills beside the road. Reuben and I looked at each other in terror as the car was lifted up and swept backward. Turning quickly, I could see Plum Creek— usually a mild, meandering stream, but now a roaring, torrential mud flow—directly behind us.

"Reuben," I screamed above the roar of the water, "we're going into the flood!"

He clutched my hand and together we murmured a prayer as we prepared to face certain drowning. As we braced ourselves, our car came to a sudden halt. Looking back I could see we had rammed into a telephone pole only a few feet in front of the raging creek. I breathed a sigh of relief and we started to get out of the car. But the doors wouldn't open! The car had sunk so far into the sand that the doors were jammed. I gasped as I looked down—our legs were caught too, pinned in the sand that was rapidly filling the inside of the car.

Terrified and helpless, Reuben and I could only sit there and let the sand pack us firmly to our waists. Meanwhile the water both outside and inside the car rose higher and higher. There was no use shouting for help; the roaring of the flood muffled everything.

As darkness set in—the blackest night I'd ever seen—the freezing air made Reuben and me shiver uncontrollably. With the lower parts of our bodies locked tight in the sand, the water continued to creep up to our necks. We held our heads as high as possible and tilted our noses back above the water. Although I tried to keep my lips tightly closed, I found myself swallowing some of the muddy slime. "O God," I prayed, "please help us. Please!"

Incredibly, just as all seemed lost, the water level began to drop and the noise of the flood seemed to lessen as well. A sense of calm came over us. But then another problem presented itself, adding to our difficulties. In our tightly sealed prison, our oxygen was now nearly gone and the door handles were buried in wet sand. Reuben and I searched for some kind of tool to break a window, but we couldn't find anything. And time was running out for us.

In that moment of complete isolation, we knew we were probably going to die. "I guess this is it," I told Reuben.

"Yes," he answered. "But we've had a good life together."

God has given us a good life, I thought. But He had always given us courage, too, courage to fight and not give up. I thought of the 46th Psalm, a favorite of mine. It said something about courage, didn't it? I began to say it aloud from memory. "God is our refuge and strength, a very present help in trouble. Therefore will we not fear, though the earth be removed, and though the mountains be carried into the midst of the sea . . ."

The words sounded so appropriate that I began repeating them, and as I did, I felt a kind of Presence enter the car, a Presence that seemed once again to remove our fear.

Just seconds later a small stone shattered the windshield. Large rocks had been hitting the car all through our ordeal—fortunately for us, not breaking the glass at the peak of the flood, which would have drowned us. Now the small stone made a hole, not a big one, but large enough to give us breath *and* hope.

A few minutes later we heard voices. Being virtually buried alive, we couldn't tell where they were coming from. Through chattering teeth, Reuben joined me as I again said the 46th Psalm. Was something about to happen?

I don't know what a guardian angel looks like, but when a man suddenly peered into our car, he surely seemed heaven-sent. Seeing our situation, the man ran for help and the next thing we knew a winch was being hooked to the front of our car. A grinding noise followed as our car top was pulled back like the lid on a can of sardines. Two men—one of them our "angel"—climbed into the car and carefully dug us out with shovels, then took us to the hospital in Englewood, Colorado.

At the hospital we were washed repeatedly, given warm blankets and hot tea and told that eastern Colorado had been hit by the worst flood in its history. The hospital was filled with injured people.

The next morning we awoke without any bad effects, and as soon as the road was opened, we returned to Castle Rock. For a week afterward, though not ill, I went about my household duties in a sort of daze. Finally one morning I came out of it.

"Reuben," I said, "it's time for us to go and buy a new car."

He chuckled. "I was just waiting for you to wake up."

I put on my raincoat, the one I had worn in the flood. Sticking my hand into the pocket, I felt something. I pulled out a stem with two leaves and a tiny, perfect white flower. How did it get there? Could that filthy flood water have washed it into my pocket? It seemed so strange.

My thoughts flashed back to that day. The telephone pole in just the right place; the huge rocks that hit our windshield without breaking it; the very small stone that broke the glass to give us needed air; the water at our nose level receding just in time; and finally that man, our "guardian angel," who came at the crucial moment.

Were those events just a long line of coincidences? I looked down at the little flower in my hand—and I knew they weren't. The events were miracles, God's miracles. He had been with us all along. He had given us strength and refuge when we needed it, and He had given us the biggest miracle of all— courage to face death itself without being afraid.

—*Priscilla Oman*

The Tractor Moved

"Ask, and it shall be given you," Jesus said (Matthew 7:7). I've always believed this, but never so totally as the day of the accident in 1978.

I was seventy-five years old. The grass on our 121-acre dairy farm needed cutting, so I hitched a set of mower blades to my tractor and went to work. The tractor was huge, and for added traction on our up-and-down Maryland terrain, its rear wheels were filled with five hundred pounds of fluid, and a two hundred-pound weight hung from each hub.

When I finished the job, I was on a slight uphill grade near our chicken house. I switched off the ignition and climbed down from the high seat. I was unfastening the mower blades when the tractor started moving backward.

I tried to twist around and jump up on the seat, but I didn't make it. The tractor's drawbar hit me in the knees, knocking me flat, and the seven hundred-pound left wheel rolled over my chest and stopped on top of it. I struggled for breath. The pain was agonizing. I knew I was facing death, and I made my request.

"Please, God," I begged, "release me."

At that moment the tractor began to move.

It went forward enough to free my chest, and—to my astonishment—it moved *uphill!*

My dog, and then a farmhand, found me; and after six broken ribs, two fractures and twelve days in the hospital I was back home, talking with the Maryland state trooper called to investigate the accident. "I won't try to explain it officially," he told me. "Why, a dozen men couldn't have moved that tractor off you."

Twelve men or twelve hundred, it didn't matter. Asking God's help did.

—*Lloyd B. Wilhide*

The Runaway Bus

Elmer Hambaugh will never forget that Easter weekend shortly after he became a Christian. Especially that Monday morning when the doctors came to operate on his foot.

Good Friday morning, thinking to take a short work break, Elmer parked the city bus he drove for a living in front of a suburban Cincinnati police station. As he chatted inside, Elmer was dumbstruck to see his empty bus start to roll slowly downhill, straight for an intersection packed with rush hour traffic.

He raced out, praying, *Dear God, stop that bus!* In an absurdly heroic effort, Elmer grabbed hold of a side-panel advertisement on the vehicle and dug in his heels—only to be knocked down and dragged under the chassis, one foot caught wedge-like between a rolling rear wheel and the pavement.

And then, for no apparent reason, the bus came to a halt.

There it stood, neatly parked at a crosswalk, safe behind the white line. A city maintenance worker—a man who'd never driven a bus—rushed to Elmer's rescue and managed to back up the vehicle.

Doctors at the hospital shook their heads when they saw Elmer's lacerated flesh and mangled foot. Anticipating a complicated skin graft, they scheduled a Monday morning operation.

All weekend Elmer prayed and fasted, stoic about his own pain as he concentrated on Christ's greater torment. And on Easter Monday he heard the doctors' words of amazement, words that told of something even stranger than the fact of the bus having been suddenly stopped.

"Your foot has healed. There's no reason to operate."

—*The Editors*

"Go See Nellie May"

I'd been selling cosmetics and delivering orders to people in their homes all day and I was tired and achy. Just out of bed from an attack of flu, I knew I should hurry home. But a few blocks from our street, I stopped. I thought of another customer, Nellie May White, a sweet retired schoolteacher I've known all my life. *Go see her,* something seemed to say to me.

I tapped at Nellie May's door. No answer.

I knocked again. Usually, I only had to rap once. No answer. I wanted to turn and leave, but my feet seemed glued to that porch.

I knocked a third time, and now, at last, Nellie May opened the door and invited me in. I gave her the cosmetics she'd ordered and she paid me. How pale she seemed. How unsteady on her feet she was.

"Come into the kitchen, my dear," she said, and as I followed her down the hall, I thought there was something strange about the air I was breathing.

"Now," she said, taking out a checkbook, "how much do I owe you?"

"Nellie May, you just paid me!" Then, without wasting another second, I sniffed the air and followed the faint, acrid odor into the dining room. The gas log in the fireplace there was turned on, and the flame had gone out. I could smell lethal fumes seeping from it.

We got out fast. I took Nellie May to a doctor, who immediately hospitalized her.

"I don't know how you happened along just when you did," she said later.

I do.

—*Mary Jane Hicks*

The Pencil

It was a cold midwinter day in South Carolina, but I was busy—and warm—inside the house I had lived in alone for the past fifteen years. I needed some wrapping paper, so I pulled down the folding stairs and started climbing to the attic. I was eighty-one at the time, and the moment the frigid attic air hit me I knew I should have put on a coat. Oh well, I'd hurry.

To keep the warm air downstairs, I shut the door to the attic storage room behind me. I heard a click. I knew immediately that I was locked in. The door had no knob; I'd taken it off to replace a broken one downstairs. And there was no one else in the house.

The cold penetrated my bones. I wrapped myself in a blanket to stop my shaking and looked out the attic window. No neighbors in sight. Anyway, the window was stuck shut from years of disuse.

An hour passed . . . then another. "Dear Lord, please send my children to help me." I knew this prayer was unrealistic. None of my four children was due to visit.

At my feet sat a yellowed and dusty pile of my son Billy's school papers. On top of them lay an old pencil. I picked it up, thinking of the hours it had spent in Billy's hand.

Once again I prayed for help. Immediately, as clear as any words I've ever heard, a question came to me, "What is that in thy hand?"

I looked at the pencil, my glance falling not on the leaded end, but on the metal end that had once held an eraser. It was now flattened, no doubt by my Billy's biting down as he sought to unlock a math problem.

I went to the door and inserted this end of the pencil into the keyhole. The lock turned. The door opened.

—*Mrs. Theo Hill*

Take-Home Chicken

Tuesday night was chicken night at the restaurant where I worked as a waitress, but on this Tuesday few customers ordered it. "Take some home," said the manager. The chicken was greasy, so I wrapped it in plastic, a box and a bag.

The last customers lingered, and we closed late. Missing the last bus, I began walking home through deserted Milwaukee streets. Unable to afford a cab, I prayed and sang a hymn. God would see me home safely.

But He didn't. A man with a knife leaped out of the shadows, pushed me down a dark side street, and spoke in ugly language of what he'd do when we reached his place on Brady Street. Why had God forsaken me?

Despite my anger, I kept praying. And then, out of nowhere I heard four words. They were very clear, very firm. "Debbie, eat your chicken." What? Was I losing my mind? "Debbie, eat your chicken."

As I was being dragged along, I pulled out a chicken breast, struggling with all the wrappings. Crying too hard to eat, I just carried it in my hand. We reached Brady Street.

Two large dogs rummaged in spilled trash cans. Suddenly the dogs perked up their heads, sniffed the air. Growling, baring teeth, they charged at us. My attacker fled.

The dogs did not lunge at me. They fixed their eyes on the chicken in my hand. I tore off meat and threw it down, where they fought hungrily for it.

Dropping pieces every few yards, I got the stray dogs to follow me home. By the time I was safely inside I'd begun to understand. *Debbie, eat your chicken*—the chicken that had been wrapped too thickly to be smelled by even a dog. But in my hand . . .

—*Deborah Rose*

What Is That in Your Hand?

Today when I am old
I look at my hand,
Wrinkled, arthritic,
Trembling, empty.
But God says,
"What is that in your hand?"
I hold it out and look again.
And lo, it is so filled with His gift
That I cup my two hands together,
And still they overflow
With His love for me to share
With others.

—*Dorothy A. Stickell*

Caught in the Train Tracks

It was 5:30 when my three children and I left the grocery store, so in order to be home before dark, we took the short-cut. A cold mist fell—the dreariness of a February dusk in Michigan.

When we came to the train tracks, my six-year-old, Lynda, tripped and fell, and her right foot became wedged between the wooden tie and the steel track.

"Untie your shoe, honey, and slip your foot out," I said. But Lynda had already pulled her shoelace into a tight knot. I tried to unravel the knot with my house key, then a hairpin. Still it held fast. I tried yanking Lynda's foot free of the shoe, but it wouldn't come. I had to get the knot untied.

Starting to worry, I scooted my other two children down the embankment, then dropped my bag of groceries and ran back to Lynda.

Just then I felt a faint vibration. An approaching train! I dug at the knot—ripping my nails, bloodying my fingers. Lynda and I both broke into fearful sobbing.

"O God," I cried, "help us. Please, God."

Two little faces stared up at me from the ditch, terror-stricken. My eyes then strayed to the spilled bag of groceries.

"The ham! The ham!" I screamed in a strange fit of revelation. I grabbed the canned ham, ripped the key from its bottom and peeled off the lid. Using the sharp edge of the lid, I severed the shoelace and pulled Lynda out of her shoe. In the glare and roar of the oncoming train we tumbled into the ditch. Safe.

Now, I've heard it said that God gives us what we need when we need it. But I've since wondered, what did the Lord give me just then? The sharp lid on a can of ham, or an imagination sharpened to the quick?

—Helen S. McCutcheon

A Cry of Help

My minister-father believed that God walked beside you day by day, lending you a hand whenever you needed it. He shared this faith with his four children.

I remember one summer night about nine o'clock when we were all returning from a day's outing in the family jalopy. Suddenly a car with glaring headlights swerved around the bend, sideswiping our car. My father, blinded by the headlights, veered off the road, crashed through a fence and came to a sudden stop. Our car was leaning precariously toward the right.

"Don't anyone move," Dad warned. "We don't know what's below us. Just sit still until someone comes to help. God is with us."

We scarcely dared breathe. We were even afraid to call for help. Dad said the noise might make the car lean still further. My baby sister slept in mother's lap. Time dragged on. Cars whizzed by us on the highway. Nobody stopped even though our headlights were on.

When my little brother began to whimper, Dad said quietly, "Just hang on. Help will come. All of you pray."

Soon the baby woke up and started to scream. Mother couldn't quiet her. We heard a car drive by slowly, slam on its brakes and stop. Our ears strained as a car door opened and then footsteps approached.

"Great guns," a man exclaimed when he saw all of us in the car. "I'll go get help. There's a garage nearby." The tone of his voice frightened me as he added, "Don't anyone move!"

He disappeared but soon returned with another man and a tow truck. In no time at all we were safely back on the road.

"You're lucky to be alive. There's a river about thirty feet below that fence you crashed through," the garage man explained. "One little move in the wrong direction and you all would have been pitched right into it."

"If your windows hadn't been open," said our benefactor, "I never would have heard that baby and figured something was wrong."

"The Lord was with us," said my father.

That night, and for many nights, our family prayers were words of gratitude to God for watching over us.

—*Karin Asbrand*

Prayer Is Power

Prayer is reaching
   beyond human scope,
Past reason, past logic,
   past yearning, past hope.
Available always
   through faith every minute;
Prayer is a power
   with miracles in it.

—*Viola Jacobson Berg*

When I Stopped to Pray

When four-year-old Charles Odam, a neighbor's son, strayed from home, everyone in our heavily wooded, rural area pitched in to look for him. After checking out a big, deep spring I climbed the mountainside, calling the boy and listening. No answer.

At the top of the mountain, green moss grew in a thick carpet on the woodland floor and late afternoon sunlight glimmered through the trees. I dropped to my knees and prayed to God for His help. Raising my head, I noticed a faint trail I had never seen before—just a trace used by forest animals.

An enticing trail for a little boy! But it ended where someone had cut logs. No sign of Charles there. The sun was going down. Time to go back. Just then I heard a wild animal's cry, a little "miaow" like a bobcat's kitten. Again it came. I peered through some bushes. There was Charles! He'd cried till he could only make that funny little sound. He locked his arms around my neck and I carried him all the way home. On the way, I thought about the hidden trail. What if I hadn't bowed my head to pray?

—Nadine Moody

The Divine Quiet

Slap! slap! slap! slap! Waves battered the gas cans we clung to. Rain drummed on our faces. Lightning slashed the black sky over our heads. In the six hours since Kenya's huge Lake Naivasha had swallowed our boat during a sudden storm, my wife, Doris, and I and our friend Jerry Piercey had been laboring in the water, praying, believing we could reach safety by kicking our makeshift floats toward shore. But the wind and waves kept changing direction. In the chilly lake our bodies were becoming numb. Hypothermia. Jerry was going into shock, his face sagging toward the water.

Yet I knew that people from the hotel were looking for us. I'd even seen the lights of their boat. But even now, as the boat came near, our screams were being drowned by the craft's powerful motor. *Drowned.* I looked at Doris struggling to hold on to the gas can and keep her head above water. Our eyes held. She cried out, "I rebuke you, Satan, in the name of Jesus, for trying to kill us! I claim victory through the blood of Jesus!"

"Amen," I shouted with all my puny strength. And one more time, "Help!"

Slap! slap! Only the waves answered. But then, a different sound, the snort of a motor starting, then a steady rumble, drawing closer and closer. In minutes, rescuers were dragging our exhausted bodies into the boat.

A split second before I'd made that last cry, a submerged log had sheared a pin from the boat's propeller. The helmsman had turned off the motor to replace it.

That's how, in the quiet, the divine quiet, my last cry had been heard.

—Harry B. Garvin

Overboard!

I remember how badly our kids wanted to go fishing with us that November morning. The two boys tried to talk us into letting them skip school, and even the little girl was for it. But of course we said no.

My wife and I always went fishing Mondays. I'd shut down my filling station and we'd haul our outboard to Lake Chickamauga, north of Chattanooga. This particular Monday was gray and raw. But that meant good fishing, and we'd have the lake to ourselves.

Sure enough, when we reached the beach there wasn't another car or boat in sight. We pushed the boat into the water, I got the motor going, and we were off, without so much as a frown over the fact that Vivian couldn't swim a stroke and wasn't wearing a life jacket. Funny how you figure some things just won't happen to you.

Vivian had brought a coat for me to put on, but I couldn't take time before starting. Seems like I couldn't wait to get to a spot I knew where I could just smell those big black bass waiting for us. Out on the water, though, it was a lot colder. We were moving along pretty good, maybe eighteen miles per hour, and the wind was fresh.

"You'll catch cold!" Vivian hollered over the noise the outboard was making.

Well, I reached for the coat, and I guess I gave the tiller a twist, because that boat gave a terrific lurch. I was holding on so I didn't fall. But Vivian was thrown from the seat into the water.

I choked the motor down, never taking my eyes off the spot where she went under. Then I dived. I swam straight down, looking for her through the brown water. I saw her, got my arm around her and started kicking for the surface. We broke water just when I thought my lungs would burst.

Vivian was wonderful. She didn't fight me or grab me the way some people will, just lay back on my arm and I saw she was praying. I looked around for the boat. I couldn't hold her up much longer with our heavy clothes full of water.

I couldn't see the boat. I turned around the other way, figuring the dive had mixed me up. I made a compete circle in the water. There was no boat. Then I saw it. It was two hundred yards from us and moving away fast. In my hurry to get in the water I hadn't shut down the motor all the way. The boat was gone and so were we.

I saw Vivian had seen it now, too, but she just whispered, "God's going to take care of us, Bennie."

Well, I knew *I* couldn't take care of us much longer, that was sure. The shore looked a million miles away. There wasn't a sign of anyone else on the beach, and even if someone came right now, by the time they could put a boat in the water and get out to us, it was going to be too late.

It was the weight of our clothes, plus the ice-cold water, that made it so bad. I knew we had to get Vivian's coat off. I got my arms under her shoulders and she wiggled and tugged at the heavy, clinging thing, and we both swallowed a lot of water. But at last she broke free of it.

But getting my boots off was a different thing. I had on the high-laced shoes I wore at the filling station and they got heavy as iron and dragged me down. I tried to get one hand down to undo the laces, but we both got ducked. Vivian had had all the water she could take.

She wasn't scared, though, not even now. "God's going to help us," she said, over and over.

Well, Vivian seemed so sure I began to figure how maybe God could do it. Perhaps He could send a seaplane and set it down on the water beside us. But the only thing in that gray winter sky were a few birds.

I was too tired to hold my head out of the water all the time. I sank down below the surface where I didn't have to kick too hard in those iron boots, holding Vivian up above me. Every little while I climbed up and got a swallow of air. Each time it seemed like I wouldn't make it.

Then I knew I was dying, because I could see my whole past life. And it wasn't much to look at. Not until two years ago, anyway. I saw the years I'd spent stock car racing, the money I'd wasted, the heavy drinking, the close calls racing a car after a few drinks.

And I saw Vivian, the way she'd been all those years. She'd never given up on me, she'd just kept on praying for me. No matter how late or how drunk I'd come home, she'd have dinner hot and waiting. And no cross words either, just:

"God loves you, Bennie. He's waiting for you."

Then one night, two years ago, I'd come home at 2:00 A.M. when the bars closed, and there was Vivian just sitting and waiting like she always was. And suddenly I knew she was right about God because no one could be as good as Vivian on his own. I got down on my knees then and there and gave my life to Him . . .

I swam up to the air and breathed for a while, remembering these things and the wonderful family life we'd had ever since. I hauled one of my boots up as far as I could and clawed at the laces again, but they were hard as steel. I sank back below the water. I didn't think I'd make it to the top again. My arms ached with holding Vivian above me.

Well, it was God's life now and it was all right for Him to take it anytime. I just didn't like to think about the kids, coming home from school, and us not there. I was too tired, too tired to keep struggling. I thought I could sleep—except that Vivian was pulling at me, tugging my arm. She was shouting:

"The boat! The boat!"

Now I saw something moving on the lake. I couldn't make out what it was at first, but it looked like it was coming nearer.

"It's the boat!" Vivian said.

It couldn't be. But it was, our own empty boat, somehow turned around and headed straight for us. I knew it couldn't happen. But I was seeing it. And even then I didn't dare hope I could grab it. I didn't have any swim left. That boat would have to come to the very square foot of water where we were for it to do us any good. If it was even three feet away it was going to pass us by.

I watched it come, moving straight as if a sure hand was on the tiller. And suddenly I knew—sure as I'd ever known anything—that that boat was coming right to us.

I just lifted up my hand and my fingers closed over the side of it. It was the last strength I had. I couldn't do any more for a long while than just hold on. Vivian had more strength than I had by then. She climbed aboard and shut the motor down, and for a long time I just hung on. Then, when I was rested a bit, I climbed in too.

Well, we sat there, water streaming off us, and we just shouted for joy. Then we sang for joy. Then we prayed for joy and just magnified God in every way we knew. Vivian saw I was rubbing my arms and she said:

"Bennie, it wasn't God alone. You held me up until He could come."

But I shook my head. "You've held me up too, Viv. I was thinking in the water how you prayed for me all those years when I couldn't. Well, I was just swimming for you, when you couldn't."

And I guess that's about all we can do for each other, just hold one another up, until God provides the help we need.
                                                                    —*Bennie Shipp*

The Extension Phone

A few years ago, my wife, Betty, and I had a work day around the house. She was painting a room and I was cleaning up the basement. At noon, as we had lunch, I leafed through the mail. "Phone bill's high," I said. "This time for sure, let's really get rid of that basement extension instead of just talking about it."

Betty agreed. When we'd moved into our house in 1980 we'd had three phones installed—in the bedroom, in the kitchen, and one in the basement which we never used.

We cleaned up the dishes and Betty sighed. "I must have overdone it," she said. "I feel kind of tired. I think I'll go upstairs and rest awhile."

I went back to the basement. I don't know how long I puttered away before the phone rang. I hesitated, expecting Betty to answer. But she didn't. Strange. For the first time that I could remember, I stepped over to the extension. "Hello?"

"This is the operator." The voice was terse. "Your wife is ill. She's upstairs. Hurry!"

I dashed up two flights. Betty lay on our bed, racked with convulsive chills, almost unconscious. I managed to get her into the car and we raced to the hospital. Doctors worked to control her temperature, raging at nearly 105 degrees. It took five days to stabilize her condition—caused by noxious fumes that had collected as she worked in a small room using oil-based paint.

"I knew I was sinking," Betty explained when she was able. "I made a grab at the phone, dialed 0, and asked the operator to ring back till you answered."

On a phone that almost didn't exist.

—*Dick Schneider*

"Send Some of Your Angels"

In the late 1940s my husband, Frank, and I were driving late at night on a deserted road in the mountains near Chattanooga when we had a flat tire. Because of the rocky road edge, Frank was unable to brace the car and change the tire. Out of the night a car appeared. Two of the biggest, roughest-looking bearded men I'd ever seen got out. With powerful hands they steadied the car, swiftly changed the tire, and drove off. They had not uttered a word.

In 1952, Frank was a naval officer stationed in Europe. We were driving with our family through thick fog in the Swiss Alps when a gap in the road, about six feet wide and four feet deep, confronted us. Night was coming on, so Frank walked the others down to the next village. Since all our belongings were in the car, I stayed behind. I waited. Nervously I tried to pray. The words of Psalm 91:11–12 came to mind: "For he shall give his angels charge over thee . . . They shall bear thee up in their hands . . ." And then I blurted out, "Lord, *send some of Your angels.* Please."

A truck suddenly appeared. Out of it piled six big, rough-looking bearded men. Without speaking, they picked up their truck and carried it across the washout. Then with strong, powerful hands they picked up *my* car—with me in it—carried it across the trench, and set it safely on the other side. They never said a word, and disappeared into the night.

I drove into the village of Brig, where I found my family. Nobody in the village could imagine who those men were. All I knew was that they had come, and they had borne me up "in their hands."

Who are these silent men? Will they have reason to help us—again?

—*Mary Hattan Bogart*

"Someone Pulled Me Out"

We were standing in my parents' front yard saying good-bye when we heard her scream—it was our little daughter, two and a half. Rushing to the backyard, we found Helen standing in the center of the flagstone sidewalk, crying and dripping wet. It was apparent that she had fallen into my parents' small but deep fish pond. Thank God she was safe!

Then, as my wife rushed over to pick Helen up, it hit me. I couldn't see any wet footprints anywhere around the pond, yet our baby was standing a good twenty feet away from the water. The only water was the puddle where she stood dripping. And there was no way a toddler could have climbed out of the pool by herself—it was six or seven feet in diameter and about four feet deep.

As Helen grew up, we often puzzled over those strange circumstances. She herself had no memory of the event; she was, however, haunted by an intense fear of water.

Many years later, when Helen and her soldier husband were living in San Antonio, she began to work through that fear with the help of an army chaplain, Pastor Claude Ingram. After spiritual counseling and prayer sessions, he asked her to go back in memory and relive the frightening fish pond experience. She put herself in the scene again and began describing the pond and the fish in detail. She cried out as she relived the moment of falling into the water. Then suddenly Helen gasped. "Now I remember!" she said. "He grabbed me by the shoulders and lifted me out!"

"Who did?" asked Pastor Ingram.

"Someone in white," she answered. "Someone pulled me out, then left."

—*William T. Porter*

Out of the Storm

I didn't expect the storm to break until later that day. When the sky cracked open and the rains began, I was still driving on the main road with my granddaughter, MaryBeth. The wind howled, swirling bits of sagebrush around my little car, and I peered anxiously out of the windshield. My farm in Arnegard was still twelve miles away! Then I remembered the shortcut around some grazing land.

It was a gravel road, deeply rutted by tractor marks, as is common in these rural parts of North Dakota. Something warned me not to risk it, but darkness was coming on and I was anxious to get home. I came to the fork and turned off the paved road.

"How did your practice go, MaryBeth?" I asked brightly. I knew my ten-year-old granddaughter was deathly afraid of storms. She had come to spend the Easter holiday with me and, to pass the time, had joined the church choir. Tomorrow, Easter Sunday, they would be singing the beautiful "Hallelujah Chorus" from Handel's *Messiah.*

"It was fine, Grandma," MaryBeth said in a small voice, keeping her eyes on the road.

I zigzagged along, grumbling each time I swerved to miss the giant cuts of the tractors. Then suddenly, as I rounded a curve, a blur of lights exploded in front of me. Horrified, I pulled hard on the wheel. A big car *swooshed* by, crowding us into a deep rut. The steering wheel jerked out of my hands and the car flipped over. We rolled over one more time into the roadside ditch. Then an eerie stillness filled the car except for the furious drumming of the rain . . .

Dazed, I tried to move myself. The crash had pushed me under the steering wheel and into the leg space in front of the driver's seat. I heard a weak whimper from the back seat. "Are you hurt, child?" I called.

There was a brief silence. Then a faint voice said, "I think I'm okay, Grandma."

I remembered stories I had heard of cars bursting into flames with the occupants trapped inside. "Come to me if you can," I called frantically. I knew I was too hurt to move to her. My legs were twisted and there was a strange heaviness in my chest.

The car had landed on its roof and MaryBeth had to crawl along it, pushing aside the seat cushions that had come loose and blocked her way. In a few moments I saw her frightened face peering at me from between the spokes of the steering wheel.

"Lord, forgive me for bringing this upon her," I groaned to myself. But there was no time to chide myself for choosing the shortcut. I had to think of a way to get help. Should I send my frightened granddaughter out in the rain where lightning flashes cracked across the sky? There was little chance of another car coming by and seeing us because we were hidden from the road. Dismally, I recalled that my husband wouldn't return from a business trip until tomorrow. The rest of my family wouldn't come by until it was time for tomorrow's church service. There was only one solution. MaryBeth would have to go out in the storm that terrified her and look for help.

My eyes searched the car for an opening. Just before the crash, MaryBeth had partially cranked down her steamed-up window to see out, and it was still open. "Crawl through the window, child," I told her feebly.

Soon she managed to wiggle out into the rain. "I'm scared, Grandma," she wailed through the wind and thunder crashes.

"Don't be frightened," I called. "Look for a light or a house." There was silence. Then at last she said, "I think I see some lights!"

"Go to them," I urged, and prayed for God to be with her as she splashed off through the fields.

I tried to free myself, but it was useless. The pain in my legs and chest was becoming unbearable, and I had to rest my head against the steering wheel for support. "Dear God, please protect and guide MaryBeth," I prayed over and over again. "Send Your guardian angel to be with her!"

The rain continued to pour on the crushed car as I waited

and prayed. It seemed like hours and hours. What had happened to MaryBeth? Had she found someone? Was she lost in the storm?

Faith had always been strong in my family. We came to the farm lands three generations ago from Norway, and had always lived by the land and our faith. "My faith looks up to Thee, Thou Lamb of Calvary," I repeated to myself over and over.

I don't know how long I lay in the car, praying. But suddenly through the steady movement of the rain and wind I began to detect a new motion. What was it—a rubbing? Craning my neck painfully, I was able to see cows nudging my wrecked car!

"Hiyah, hiyah! Get home, you critters," I heard someone shouting. *It's a farmer,* I thought joyfully. I began to call for help.

"What's that?" came a startled reply from out in the storm. Soon a rain-soaked farmer was peering through the opened window of my car. I tried to smile at him. "Are you hurt?" he cried, vainly trying to pull open the jammed door.

"Somewhat," I answered weakly. "But I can't move and had to send a little girl for help. She's out there somewhere . . ." I looked helplessly into the fields.

"Don't worry," the man said. "We found her in my field. My cattle strayed in the storm and I found her right in the middle of my cows. She was so frightened and exhausted that she wasn't able to make any sense, so I brought her back to my house. Then I came on horseback to round up the cattle, and found you." He shook his head. "It's amazing. I wouldn't have seen a darn thing in this storm if it weren't for these here cows!"

Suddenly I knew how the Lord had answered my prayers. *He had sent the cows!* They were our guardian angels—a herd of cows!

The farmer took off his horse's saddle blanket and covered me with it, promising to go for help. Soon I was taken to Arnegard Hospital. MaryBeth, already there, rushed to my side.

"You'll be all right now, Grandma," she said happily.

I nodded, thinking about God's special answer to my

prayers. My old body would mend. MaryBeth was safe. She would still be able to sing that wonderful song of praise at the Easter service.

"Yes, child," I said to her, "the 'Hallelujah Chorus' will surely be sung in church tomorrow!"

—Emma Stenehjem

A Horse Called Amber

This is a story of two horses, one a jet-black mare called Midnight—some would call her a "devil horse"—and the other, my favorite, a gentle six-year-old palomino called Amber.

Shortly after my husband, John, had bought Midnight, I went out to work with her. I led her out, locked the stable door behind me, and proceeded to saddle and mount her. Midnight was nervous. She skittered. Within seconds she became violent. She reared and threw me to the ground, then went berserk, rushing wildly about the yard. Suddenly she headed back to me at full gallop, teeth bared. Already in great pain from a shattered neck joint, unable to move, I knew she was trying to kill me, to stomp me to death. *"Lord, Lord,"* I screamed, but there was no one near to hear.

No one human, that is. Unbelievably, Amber came charging out of the stable. She hurled herself at Midnight, savaging her with her teeth. Midnight retreated, charged again, retreated again and came back again. Amber stood her ground, defending me until Midnight gave up.

And to think that I'd last seen Amber in her stall, a restraining chain across its entrance. And the stable door—it was locked. I myself had carefully slipped the metal bolt.

Yet my gentle Amber had rescued me. She had overcome the barriers between me and her. Had done that with crucial and uncanny speed.

How?

—Mary D. Wilson

Out of the Night

Christmas Day
1944

Dear Mom,

   This is a very different Christmas Day than I have ever spent
in my life. Right now I'm living in the hayloft of a farmer's barn,
and I'm very glad to be here rather than out in a foxhole
somewhere . . .

The Battle of the Bulge. The final desperate attempt of the
Germans to break through Allied lines in Belgium and dash
to Antwerp and the sea. For six days our 84th Infantry Division had been diverted from the Ninth Army in the north to
the beleaguered First Army area in the Ardennes forest. The
fiercest fighting of the war, and I, a nineteen-year-old private,
was in the middle of it.

My letter home to Pennsylvania was written on a Christmas
morning that was sunny and quiet—deceptively quiet. "The
barn I slept in last night," I wrote, "made me think of the place
where Jesus came into the world." Then I began reminiscing
to Mom about the good Christmases we'd had as I was growing up—always starting with the traditional dawn service at St.
John's Lutheran in Boyertown. Church had always been an
important part of my life. I'd started college thinking I might
go into the ministry.

The letter home was upbeat all the way. I didn't mention
anything about the things that had been troubling me. How
I had become disillusioned with organized religion because I
saw so few Christians either at home or in the combat zone—
certainly not Christians trying to live the way Jesus had taught.
Or how the weather had been so miserable and the fighting
so blazing that I feared I'd never live to see Pennsylvania
again.

The last straw was my being sent to these snow-covered hills
and woods where we might be attacked at any moment from
out there, somewhere. I was beginning to think that God had
forsaken me.

Still, even though we'd spent the last five days floundering
around trying to stop the Germans, even though our supply

trucks had been captured, at least we'd had a barn for shelter on Christmas Eve, and our cooks were promising us a hot meal for Christmas Day.

"Let's go, men," Sergeant Presto, our squad leader, shouted. "Collect your gear and fall out. We're going on a mission."

I groaned. We all groaned. There went our first hot meal in a week!

We drove for about ten miles and then the trucks dropped us and sped away. It was dusk. Troops were strung out all along a dirt road that circled through some hills. When Presto came back from a meeting with the platoon leader, he gathered the ten of us—we were one man short in the squad—around him.

"Okay, men, here's what we're going to do. This won't take long and we're going to travel light. Leave your packs and entrenching tools here." He made it sound so simple. Intelligence had said that some German infantry were dug into a nearby hill and were causing havoc by shooting down on the roads in the area. Our battalion's job was to go up and flush them out.

Single file on each side of the winding road, we moved up the hill. We moved quietly, warily. At the top, we were surprised to find, not Germans, but an abandoned château in the middle of a clearing. Our squad went into the building. We found a billiard table and the tension broke as we played an imaginary game of pool using our rifles as cues.

Then Presto came stalking in. The Germans, he said, were in the woods beyond the clearing. Our orders were to chase them out into the waiting arms of another battalion positioned at the other end of the woods.

"There'll be three companies in this deal," Presto said. "Two of us will stretch out along the edge of the forest while the other hangs back in reserve. Now, as soon as we push into the woods, everybody fires, got it?"

We spread out, walked through the darkness to the forest's edge, then, at a signal, we burst in, opening up with everything we had. We kept up a brisk pace, keeping contact with our buddies along the moving line, walking and firing for about

a mile. But the forest was empty. There was no movement
anywhere . . .

The trees in front of us exploded. Suddenly, the night went
bright with every kind of firing I'd ever seen or heard of—
rifles, rifle-launched grenades, mortars, machine guns, tracers
over our heads, bullets at our thighs. But worst of all, Tiger
tanks. At least six of them, opening up point-blank with 88-
millimeter cannons. Their projectiles whined and crashed all
up and down our line.

Our intelligence was wrong, I thought angrily, as I flung myself
down on my stomach. *They told us there were no tanks up here.
Now we're really in for it.*

Within seconds men were screaming in pain all around me.
I saw a tree with a big trunk and made a sudden lunge to get
behind it, but I wasn't quick enough. Something tore into my
thigh. There was hot, searing pain.

We were completely pinned down. The Tiger tanks kept
scanning their turrets and firing on every yard of our line. The
German ground troops sent their small arms fire into anything
that moved.

The minutes went by. Five. Ten. Fifteen. Then came a lull
in the barrage. I called over to my best buddy, Kane. We
called him "Killer." He was the gentlest guy in our platoon,
but we'd nicknamed him that after the popular comic strip
character, "Killer Kane."

"Are you hurt, Killer?"

"Naw. But I think everybody else over here is. Presto's hit
bad."

I called to Cruz on my right. He was our squad's B.A.R.
man. There was no answer. Then I barely heard him whispering, "I'm hurt. Real bad. Floyd's dead. Corporal John's hit
bad."

Well, I thought, *if Presto's out and the Corporal, too, we don't
have a leader.*

The pounding started again, this time with flares so they
could spot us better. We did some firing back and then the
action subsided into another lull.

Down along the rear of our line came a figure, crawling. It
was our platoon runner. "Captain says we're getting no-

where," he whispered to Killer and me. "We're pulling back
in five minutes. Move out when you hear our covering fire."

I crawled over to Killer. "We've got to get our guys out of
here," I said. "You go up your side and I'll go down mine,
and we'll drag as many as possible to that big tree back there."

"How're we going to get them out of here, though?"

"I don't know," I said. "But we can't leave them lying
here."

We were trapped. I lay there on the cold ground feeling
helpless, that forsaken feeling again. Where was the God that
I had prayed to during all those years of church and Sunday
school back home in Pennsylvania? "And whatsoever ye shall
ask in my name, that will I do," the Bible had said to me clearly
(John 14:13). Was it necessary, when I needed help so badly,
to ask?

"O Lord," I mumbled, "help us. We're trying to get our
wounded buddies out of here. Show us the way."

I had no sooner started dragging Corporal John toward the
meeting tree when the firing started up in the center of our
line. *There's the signal for pulling back,* I thought frantically, *but
we can't do it. The Germans will sweep in on us; they'll mop us up
before we can pull back.*

Just as I got to the tree, I saw that Killer had brought back
three wounded squad members. So we had six in all to get
back. I closed my eyes and in desperation said: "In Your name,
Lord, help us."

I opened my eyes. In the black of night, moving mysteriously among the shattered trees, a giant hulk came toward us.
The Germans, my heart thumped, *they've broken out of the brush.
They're bearing down on us.* No, it was something else, something unbelievable. It now came into full view and stopped
beside our tree.

A horse.

A big, docile, shaggy chestnut, standing there without a
harness, as though awaiting our bidding.

Killer and I looked at each other in disbelief. We didn't
question then where the horse came from, or how, or why; we
just got to work. Moving swiftly, we draped Cruz and the
Corporal on the chestnut's broad back, then Mike and Presto.
Then, with Killer carrying one of our buddies and me carrying

the other, we led the horse out of the woods. At the clearing the horse trotted on ahead of us, straight to the château, and by the time Killer and I got there, our wounded were already on medical stretchers. The two men we carried in were cared for; the medics gave a quick look at my shrapnel wound; and then, as fast as we could, Killer and I went to find the horse. We wanted to pat him, give him some sugar, anything to make him sense our gratitude.

But he wasn't there. We looked everywhere, asked everyone we saw, but no one could tell us anything about him. He had simply vanished—gone from us as mysteriously as he had come.

The next morning at the aid station the shrapnel was removed from my leg, and at noon Killer and I lined up for our belated Christmas dinner. The day before, one hundred ninety men in our company would have answered the chow call; today there were thirty-five of us. All the wounded men in our squad had survived, however, though some were never to see action again.

Killer and I looked at the turkey and sweet potatoes in our mess kits. Hot and savory and long-awaited as this food was, we had no appetite. We were still too full of our emotions: the sorrow for lost buddies; the shock of our own survival; the strange, deeply affecting arrival and departure of the horse. We could not get the horse out of our minds then, nor have I since, for that noble creature did more than just save our lives; he reaffirmed my faith. I have always believed that on that Christmas night forty-four years ago, God sent that horse to reassure a doubting soldier of His presence, even as He had sent His Son for that purpose on a Christmas night twenty centuries ago.

—*Jack Haring*

GOD
REASSURES

*The Lord will command his lovingkindness in the daytime,
and in the night his song shall be with me,
and my prayer unto the God of my life.*

—Psalm 42:8

God knows that we need reassurance. "Fear not," He keeps telling us throughout the pages of the Bible. Even when the boat is rocking and the waves threaten to swamp us, Jesus tells us, "Don't be afraid." And He is the one who can say "Shut up" to the storm—and have everything become quiet and still.

God reassures us in many ways. He is always sending us signs of His love and care. When the Apostle Paul was preaching in Greece, he became very discouraged. But he was reassured when his friend Titus brought the good news that the Christians in Corinth were holding on to their faith (2 Corinthians 7:5–7). David found reassurance when he remembered watching a sparrow build a nest in the altar of the Tabernacle. That memory enabled him to keep going and make the vale of tears a valley of blessing (Psalm 84:1–7).

Twice in this section we are shown that God knows our name. This is a very biblical theme. The prophet Isaiah reminded the people of Israel that God knew them personally, and the promise holds true for us:

But now thus saith the Lord that created thee,
O Jacob, and he that formed thee, O Israel,
Fear not: for I have redeemed thee,
I have called thee by thy name; thou art mine.
—*Isaiah 43:1*

And as the Good Shepherd, Jesus calls all of His sheep by name (John 10:1–3).

These stories also show us that God is in charge of His world. Nothing is too small for Him to provide—shoelaces, a flower. Nothing is too hard for Him to perform—creating a pool in the desert or transforming a marriage. In little ways and in large, He demonstrates His tender care for His children. We never need to doubt His love for us.

The Everlasting Arms

When the doctor told me that my precious six-week-old son, Paul, was blind, I went into shock. I tried to pray, but for some reason I couldn't.

Hours passed and I still could not form words into prayer. Meanwhile, news of our baby's disability spread among our family, friends and church congregation. An army of prayer warriors carried their concern for Paul, my husband and me to the Lord.

Two days later, while I was bathing Paul, something almost mystical happened. Ever so quietly and gently I was reminded of the Bible verse ". . . and underneath are the everlasting arms" (Deuteronomy 33:27). I had the distinct feeling of being buoyed up, supported. And my depression began to lift.

Paul is an adult now. Though legally blind, he went to college and is employed; he can read with special magnifying glasses.

I discovered on that day long ago that even when you yourself cannot pray, the prayers of others can intercede for you. That barrage of prayers didn't change Paul's problem, but it changed me. Ever since, in good times and in bad, I've been sustained by the knowledge of His everlasting arms.

—Frieda E. Nowland

Brown Shoelaces

Hurrying through the supermarket, I accidentally knocked over a display of shoelaces. Impulsively, in my embarrassment, I flung a packet of men's shoelaces into the shopping cart and, after paying for them, tossed the shoelaces into my purse.

Then I was off to the rehabilitation hospital where I'd been visiting daily with Donald, a man whose arms and legs were paralyzed after he'd fallen from a ladder.

That day I found Donald unusually despondent. "Brenda," he said to me after we'd finished our physical therapy session, "I've tried to be cheerful about all this, but sometimes I feel as though God simply doesn't care any more about what happens to me."

"You *know* He cares," I began. But I had no real answer for him. We sat in silence.

"Oh, by the way," Donald said to me later as I started to leave, "no big deal, but the nurse broke one of my shoestrings this morning. Could you get me a new pair?"

Shoestrings! I opened my purse and took out the brown pair from the supermarket. We stared at them in amazement. I bent down and laced the strings into Donald's shoes.

Shoestrings. For a pair of shoes on feet that could not move to wear them out. For a set of hands that couldn't even tie the bow.

"Donald, if God cares enough to supply you with shoestrings before you even ask," I said, "I'm certain He cares enough about you in more important ways."

A smile broke onto his face. "Yes, you're right," Donald said. "I'm sure, too."

Shoestrings. Whenever I'm discouraged, I think of them. Then I know that God cares for me, too, meticulously, intimately. Right down to the laces in my shoes.

—Brenda Minner

Day of Faith

However long and dark the night,
Day is sure to break
And children rise to laughter,
And birds to rapture wake.

However long the winter,
Spring will surely come,
Bringing gold of jonquil,
Silver of flowering plum.

However deep the sorrow,
However great the pain,

Be sure that peace will follow,
As sunlight follows rain.

—*Elizabeth Neal Wells*

Someone to Talk To

On July 4, 1945, I walked gloomily through the halls of a
Chicago YWCA. I had come to the city for a crucial ear operation. Next day I'd begin four days of preparation before surgery at St. Luke's Hospital. As a piano teacher, I was especially
frightened about the outcome—the operation was so new that
few others had had it. With no friends close by, I was lonely.
Apprehensive. *If only You would send me someone I could talk to,*
I prayed to God.

As I passed the Y's solarium, I noticed a piano and, almost
as if it were the friend I needed, I felt drawn to the keyboard.
I sat down at the piano and began to play. I played and played.
The music flowed with a spirit of its own, expressing my pent-
up feelings. At last I finished and got up to leave.

"Please, don't stop!" a voice called out. All this time,
though I hadn't noticed her, a woman had been sitting in the
far corner of the room.

We introduced ourselves and started to chat. She, too, was
a stranger in town. And she, too, it turned out, had been
through the very same surgery I was about to undergo, with
"my" doctor, at "my" hospital, exactly a year before! It was
she who reassured me about the operation that in a few days
would prove to be such a success.

She had heard my music. But Someone Else had heard my
prayer.

—*Eugenia Eason*

One Red Rose

In the mid-1960s my husband's sister Muriel became very ill. My husband and six-year-old daughter, Linda, and I traveled to Tulsa to be present while Muriel underwent emergency surgery for a diseased kidney. As we neared Tulsa, a thought flashed into my mind out of nowhere. *One red rose,* a voice said. *Take one red rose to Muriel.* My husband agreed to stop at a florist's shop. However, it was late and everything was closed.

The next morning my husband went to the hospital to wait during the operation. I stayed with Linda and my husband's elderly mother at her home. All I could think of was that red rose. I felt compelled to search out that rose. So Linda and I walked uptown, and I bought one red rose.

When my husband returned, he said that Muriel had come through the surgery, and it was now touch-and-go as to whether she'd recover. He also told me he'd ordered a big bouquet of gladiolas for Muriel's room.

"That's lovely, honey," I said. "But she's *got* to have this red rose, too." When we went to the hospital later, Muriel was still groggy and wasn't able to talk to us, but I put the rose, by itself, in a vase where she could see it. Because of work commitments we had to return home without ever talking to Muriel, but we did learn that she would recover.

Soon we got a letter. "Before I went to the hospital," Muriel wrote, "I prayed that if I was supposed to live, God would send me a sign I specifically asked for, something that meant God was with me and would give me the heart to go on. When I opened my eyes after the operation, there it was, the very thing I'd prayed for—a red rose."

—*Eva Mae Ramsey*

The Newer Hope

I see a thousand miracles
With each new holy dawn,
A swiftly fading memory
Of yesterdays now gone.

I shall not dwell upon the past,
I must be moving on.

I feel God's love enfolding me;
I feel it make me strong.
I feel it lifting up my soul
Above the doubt and wrong.
And I obey Him as I run
To sing the world His song.

—*Richie Tankersley*

The Shepherd's Touch

Do you believe that God still sends extraordinary "signs" to ordinary people—as He did so often in biblical times?

I do, and so do my family and the neighbors who saw, with me, a tender—and extraordinary—expression of His love.

It came the spring after my mother's death. At seventy-six, she had been a peaceful great-grandmother, the calm, strong center of our big family network. Like my father two decades earlier, she died praising God, her faded blue eyes focused on wonderful things we couldn't see, murmuring, "Oh, it's beautiful, so beautiful."

As her oldest daughter, I had been "assistant mother" for the younger children, and that made Mother and me especially close. I grieved. But the faith that she had relied on—and nurtured in us—seemed to sustain me.

At least it did until we began, in April, to dismantle her old riverside homestead. The house had been closed for the winter, and my sister Catherine and I had set aside a few days to clean and get organized before the appraisers came to evaluate the furnishings.

That first morning in Mother's house an aching sorrow gripped me, the kind that's a long time coming and a long time going away.

As I moved through the familiar rooms with my dustcloth, mop and broom, I felt as if I were saying good-bye over and over again. Everything I saw evoked memories. Here was the butler's pantry with cupboards big enough to hide a playful little girl. Here was the west parlor with the stern-faced portraits of our ancestors that had intimidated me as a child. Here, the front hallway with the burnished, curving banister that my fingers had traced as I'd come down the staircase to be Charlie's nineteen-year-old bride.

Finally I sat down on the steps, harshly shaken, as if I'd blundered into a closed door during the night. I'd expected to feel a warm closeness to Mother in this house where I'd grown up in her care. But instead, I felt cold, diminished, shorn.

So much about me—the way I raised my children and kept house, the way I made ginger cookies, husked corn, crossed my legs at the ankles—came from her. Mother's presence in my life affirming those similarities had been a kind of security blanket. Now that was gone.

The next few days, coming back to the homestead with Catherine to finish our work, were agony. She noticed my depression, of course, and so did Charlie. Both tried, and failed, to comfort me.

On the afternoon we finished our chores, Catherine made a pot of tea and we sat down together at the big round table in the kitchen. I brooded there, chin in hand, filled with a dull, penetrating chill. *Dear Lord,* I wondered, *will I ever have those good, warm feelings again?*

Catherine leaned across the table and patted my cheek. "You look so miserable, and I don't know how to comfort you."

I shook my head and glanced around the room to avoid her sympathetic, questioning eyes. In a corner sat boxes and baskets filled with pictures, utensils and bric-a-brac to be discarded. My eyes lighted on a dingy shape. And then a very odd command marched into my head: *Go and get it.*

For a moment I stared and hesitated. What was this all about? I felt as if I were being pulled. Slowly I went over and picked up the object. It was a little statue of a lamb and mother sheep curled up together, shoulder to shoulder—the mama with her head raised high in a proud, protective way and her baby cuddled close, looking safe and loved. I brought it back to the table and sat down to study it. The bare plaster form was dull with grime.

Catherine had been watching me with puzzlement. "What's so interesting about that?"

I did not have the faintest idea. My voice said, "Are we throwing it out?"

"Why, yes, I thought we would. It's just an old knickknack that's been in the spare room ever since I can remember."

I turned it over. It was hollow and had no identifying mark inside.

Take it home and care for it, came the urging.

"I guess I'll keep it," I muttered, realizing how foolish it must seem.

That night, using a soft brush, I gently scrubbed the little animal mold in a pan of warm water and soapsuds and rinsed it carefully. The curlicues of plaster fleece were too ingrained with dust to get completely white, but the sheep and lamb figures looked much brighter. Feeling a strange stirring in my spirit, I put the statue on the dining room table and went to bed.

About six the next morning, Charlie and I came downstairs together. He opened the front door to go out on the porch for the newspaper. With a vague sense of anticipation, I went on toward the kitchen, noticing the just-awakened stillness of the new day, the fragile sunlight filtering through my lace curtains, the mellow chime of the mantel clock. As I passed through the dining room, I glanced at the statue on the table. I blinked and stood stock still.

The lamb and the ewe were covered with snowy fleece.

Dimly, I was aware that Charlie had paused beside me. "What's the matter?"

Silently I pointed.

I heard him draw a breath. I felt his fingers close around mine. At last we touched the fluff-covered animals. Their covering felt exactly like wool: It was perfectly contoured around the heads, muzzles, bodies and bobtails.

I'm not sure how long we stood there, staring at the soft, implausible mantle of whiteness that had transformed the sheep. But I do remember the understanding that came, haltingly, into my mind:

Now, just as before my mother died, I was wrapped in His miraculous enfolding love. *That* was the continuing Presence in my life, as it was in hers . . . as it would be throughout the lives of my children. No death could deprive me of *His* comfort and protection . . .

"The Lord is my Shepherd," I whispered. I felt the welcome warmth of tears on my cheeks.

During the next few days, many people saw the little statue—our children, our neighbors, some of our close relatives. Then the fleece crumbled into dust and vanished.

In the years that followed, my sons and daughters blessed me with six grandchildren, and recently a great-grandson arrived. Sometimes one or another of them will remember the story of the little statue and ask, "Do you think it was a chemical reaction, Mother?" or "Did someone play a trick on you, Nannie?"

I just smile. For I know that the Shepherd tends His sheep in wonderful, extraordinary ways.

—*Angelica Spraker Van Wie*

Hand in Hand

I'm on a guided journey,
Through this most delightful land.
I need no compass, chart or map—
God leads me by the hand.

—*Gordon Thomas*

The Leaves That Grew in Secret

Jesus tells us that when people do good things in secret, God will know about it and reward them (Matthew 6:3–4). Recently at our house we saw that happen in a fascinating way.

Nine-year-old Jill came out of her Sunday school class one blustery morning carrying a small bare tree branch and radiating enthusiasm. "See, Mom? I'm giving you a 'good deeds tree.' Every time I do something to help you, you're supposed to tape on one of these paper leaves." Her eyes sparkled. "I'm going to do *lots.*"

I gave her a hug, and when we got home I slipped the leaves in a drawer and propped the branch on a windowsill, leaning it against the glass. Some time later it must have slipped out of sight behind the curtain. Out of sight and out of mind . . .

Nothing jogged my memory until the next Sunday at the joint service following our adults' and children's Sunday school classes. "How many boys and girls have leaves on their tree branches?" the priest asked.

With a sinking feeling, I watched Jill's hand shoot up. I'd completely forgotten about the good deeds tree. Jill had been even more helpful than usual, but I hadn't added any leaves to her branch.

After church, I explained to Jill that I hadn't kept up with her good deeds. "The minute we get home we'll find that branch and I'll tape on every leaf you've earned," I told her.

As soon as we'd hung up our coats, we went to the window and I reached behind the curtain and brought out the branch. Jill began to clap her hands and bounce up and down with delight. For the branch was no longer bare, but covered with tiny, bright green *real* leaves.

Leaves of God's making.

—Sharon Addy

The Lame and the Halt

Up. Up. Up. Up. Inch by inch, stiff and headachy, I toiled up the stairs to my bedroom to get ready for my swimming lesson. The boys had been late leaving for school and now I was late, too. Snow fell implacably outside the window. *This is ridiculous,* I told myself, and plopped down on the top step. *Lord, I pleaded, when is this pain going to end? Please, can't You send me some relief?*

For five months I'd been tormented by rheumatoid arthritis—that fiendish disease that strikes at any age, from childhood on up, and sets your joints on fire—and my doctor had prescribed swimming therapy. In the water I could move quite freely, but once out of the pool I had to resume my creaking walk. I felt conspicuous and discouraged. And sorry for myself.

Now, sitting on the stairs, I wanted to give up. *What's the use?* I argued. *By the time I get there, swimming will be half over anyway.* Suddenly, a single thought shot through all my despair: *Get going!*

It was so startling that I actually pulled myself up, got into some clothes and shuffled down to the car. But before I pulled out of the driveway, which was already covered with a film of slick snow, I hesitated again. "What's the good of this?" I asked aloud.

Just go! the inner voice commanded. I went.

As I slowed to turn the corner, my eyes flicked to the left, aware of an odd movement in what looked like a large trash bag, torn open and flapping in the wind. I rolled my window down to look closer. The object moved again. Then I heard a moan, a cry for help.

"Coming," I shouted.

I opened the car door and forced my body to bend, forced it to get out and go to the dark, bundled shape in the snowdrift at the side of the street.

"Oh, thank God you're here," a small voice cried feebly.

The "bundle" was a tiny old woman who had lost her footing and fallen into the snowdrift. Her glasses, unbroken, lay a few feet away.

"I can't move," she said, her teeth chattering. "Help me."

How could I tell her that I couldn't help her up? That I couldn't even bend down to comfort her?

"I prayed," she said in a stronger voice. "I prayed you'd come along, and now here you are."

Me? For one wild moment, I wanted to laugh. How could a woman crippled with arthritis be an answer to a prayer? But there was no one else on the deserted street. It had to be me.

"O Father, be with us," I said quickly. And in one swift, effortless motion I bent down and scooped her up. In the next instant she was on her feet, picking up her glasses, smiling at me.

"Nothing broken, not even hurting," she said triumphantly, and then suddenly, we were laughing.

I drove her to her home, then went back to mine, exulting. I'd missed my swimming session, but God had given me therapy of a different kind. He had actually used me—arthritis and all—as His messenger in answering the need of another person.

Being strong for someone else had strengthened my own spirit. Now I knew I could cope.

—*Barbara Wernecke Durkin*

Flight of Faith

Regardless of weather their trip is begun;
No alibis cause a delay.
The small feathered flyers take off, rain or sun,
Heading north,
Trusting Him, day by day.

The heavenly power that makes them persist—
That guides fragile creatures like these—
Gives wings to my faith when I need an assist
And I soar
When I'm down on my knees.

—*Margaret Rorke*

The Voice on the Phone

When a tornado struck Louisville, Kentucky, in April 1974, our family was at home—all but our youngest son, Collyn. He was in kindergarten at Southern Baptist Theological Seminary a few miles away.

Huddled together in our basement, we heard the rain pounding and the storm's violent roar. When the noise abated, we went upstairs, relieved to find our neighborhood untouched. But the radio said the storm had headed toward the seminary.

My husband went for Collyn and I stayed at home with our two older boys. I tried to call the kindergarten. The number did not ring. Instead I heard clicks and then the phone went dead.

"Mama," my son Chris reported, "the radio just said the tornado went through the Baptist seminary and took the roof off."

Both children began to cry. With my own fear, how could I comfort them? I thought: *Only God can help me now. He's in charge.* "Boys," I said, "we're in God's hands."

Again I tried to phone. Dead. I was about to hang up when the number rang.

"Don't worry," said the woman who answered. "The children were taken to another building before the storm. They're fine." We hugged and shouted for joy.

The area around the seminary had been devastated. Huge trees lay twisted on the ground; live electrical wires sparked on the wet sidewalks; homeless people wandered in a daze. But my husband found Collyn safe, just as the woman had said.

Later, when I went to thank the woman who'd comforted me on the phone, Collyn's teacher said, "But Mrs. Coates, you couldn't have spoken with anyone. Our phone lines were destroyed. Besides, there was no one in the building when you called."

—*Lynne Coates*

Mrs. Joseph's Angel

"When everything's going wrong, sister," Mama used to advise me, "just stop what you're doing and scrub the kitchen or turn out a big washing. With that kind of job, you see results. It gets you going again."

That's why I'd hastily stripped the beds and gathered up damp towels that warm and gusty morning, and headed very early toward the apartment complex laundry room. I hoped I'd see no one. I didn't feel like engaging in neighborly chitchat.

For days, it seemed, things had gone maddeningly wrong.

My work, usually so satisfying, exasperated me. My closest friend seemed almost spoiling for a spat. The apartment needed cleaning, but I had little time. And now my throat felt scratchy.

Worst of all, my prayers seemed to bounce off the ceiling. I'd lost my joy, seemed headed into depression and didn't know why. *No wonder God doesn't listen,* I thought. *My problems are so tacky they bore Him. I wouldn't listen to me either!*

My self-pity lifted, however, when I discovered Mrs. Joseph, my downstairs neighbor and one of my favorite people in the world, already stuffing rose-colored tablecloths and flowered napkins into a machine. "Whatever did we do before permanent press!" she exclaimed by way of greeting.

Mrs. Joseph always delights me. I love everything about her—her flowered dresses, exquisite shoes, the music that drifts out of her windows. Her apartment is exactly like mine, but much more modern with white carpets, glass tables and accents of hyacinth blue and chrome yellow. She is seventy-nine, independent and refuses to live with any of her four middle-aged daughters.

Of course, she loves to go shopping with "the girls," take them to Bible study or to an art show. But live with one of them? Nonsense!

"I had twenty-four ladies from my church circle to tea," Mrs. Joseph explained. "My apartment is too small for that. Since old ladies like to sit down, I set up card tables. Had six tables and put a bud vase with a fresh rose on each one. It looked real pretty!"

"You're the hostess with the mostest," I smiled, my spirits rising.

"Honey, there are so many lonely people! You get to my age, everybody you know is widowed—or Lordy, Lordy, divorced!—and they mope around to beat the band. Keep moving is the secret, keep moving. Every day, find something worthwhile to do." She shook a tea towel vigorously and pitched it into the drier.

"You do get around," I admired. "I hardly ever see you anymore. What are you doing these days, Mrs. Joseph?"

"Mostly I try to help Imogene. You did hear my daughter Imogene went blind last fall?"

"No!" I simply stared at her, horrified. Shock waves hit me, and I couldn't think of what to say.

"Thank God, she's well taken care of," Mrs. Joseph answered slowly, her brown eyes filling with tears. "My girls inherited eye problems, you know. Two of them, Imogene and Rosemary, learned nearly three years ago that they might go blind."

My mind whirled as I considered the tragedy, wondering what I could offer my friend in the way of comfort. At last I asked, tentatively: "Mrs. Joseph, do you believe God heals?"

"Honey, I *know* God heals," she answered firmly. "I never questioned that. These past three years He has answered our prayers in miraculous ways. The girls got right busy and learned Braille, learned to clean house from memory, studied the Bible, did everything they could in case they lost their sight. He helped them with all of it.

"You should see Imogene get around. She's a miracle in herself, her faith and cheerfulness. Yes, God heals!" She gazed at me for a moment, seeming to decide something. "When we first got the news," she confided, "the day we all had to accept that my two girls might go blind, I thought it would kill me.

"I cried 'most all night, then woke up the next day feeling so bitter. I felt cold, cold like after Mr. Joseph died. It didn't make a piece of sense to me! I said, 'Lord, I've had a lovely, lovely life, and now I'm old. Why couldn't it be me, Lord? Why Imogene? Why Rosemary?'

"That day I asked Him just to take me on home. I cried real tears all morning, and it seemed like He didn't answer. Ah, it was a bitter time . . . I hurt till I thought it would kill me."

"How did you stand it?" I asked, deeply ashamed of my own paltry grumblings. "However did you stand it?"

She searched my face again, then replied with a question. "Do you believe in angels?"

"Yes'm, I do."

"Maybe you won't believe this, but that morning, so brokenhearted, I said, 'God, I can't even pray. You must help me with this.' You ever get where you just can't pray?" I nodded. "Well, He sent help. Honey, I heard an angel sing. It was 'Amazing Grace,' all the verses, sung over and over. It had to be an angel, 'cause there was nobody here, and it came from all over the apartment—verse after verse.

"When I heard that music I knew we'd all stand it, no matter what. I knew God would bring us through. Now I'm old, but I'm not crazy. Do you believe I heard an angel?"

I knew exactly what she'd heard, but I couldn't say a word. I simply cried and hugged her, and helped her gather her load of neatly folded linens. At the laundry room door she paused and called back to me: "Honey, God won't do those things we can do for ourselves, but when you can't do another thing, He always sends help. Call on Him and He'll answer you. Read Jeremiah thirty-three three!"

What was it she had heard? As I folded sheets and towels, I relived that day nearly three years earlier when Mrs. Joseph had anguished alone. I didn't know her then, of course, for it was the Saturday morning before I was to move into the apartment above hers.

I'd been depressed that day, too. The empty rooms echoed with loneliness. I'd brought shelf paper and cleaning supplies to busy myself as I waited for the telephone installer, but as the hours lengthened I ran out of jobs to do. Outside, a misty rain had turned into a chilly drizzle. I sat on the floor of my newly carpeted dining room, fighting off the loneliness and near-despair.

What's the point of all this? I thought. *Why bother about moving, about cleaning this stupid apartment, about anything? Who cares?* At last I prayed—honest, unadorned prayer. "God, I'm so tired of struggling. I'm so lonely. My life lacks meaning; it really doesn't matter to anyone. Help me. Please speak to me."

He spoke immediately with force and authority. "Get to your feet. Stand up. Walk through this apartment and claim it for Me. Walk through every room and praise Me for your health and strength and every good and perfect gift I have given you. Ask a blessing on every person who walks through these doors, who eats here, sleeps here, visits here." The impression, tremendously strong, could not be disobeyed. I did exactly as I was told. "Now do one more thing. Lift your voice to praise Me in song in every room of this house."

Why not? Feeling bold and a little crazy, yet filled with joy,

I walked through one room after another, singing verse after verse of my favorite hymn, "Amazing Grace." Who cared, after all? There was no one else around to hear me. For fifteen or twenty minutes I sang with all my strength.

Soon after, the phones were installed and I could leave. God had spoken to me in a very real way, and I had responded. Now I could depart in peace. The episode seemed finished.

Now I wondered, should I have told Mrs. Joseph the truth about the singing? And if so, what was the truth? Surely I'm no angel, and certainly didn't sing like one? *Or did I?* What is the truth, God? I wondered whimsically.

At once Mrs. Joseph's words returned to my mind. "God always sends help when you need it . . . don't ask Him to do what you can do for yourself . . . call on Him . . . He will answer you."

The laundry basket, piled high, felt feather-light as I hurried upstairs, eager to walk again through my apartment. In the dining room, just thinking of the kind of God who'd use me as an angel, I laughed aloud.

I wondered if Mrs. Joseph could hear me laugh. I knew He did.

—*Charlotte Hale Allen*

The Angel of Washington Square

Finally, the words, "I now pronounce you man and wife." The ceremony was over. Mike took my arm and we walked down the aisle. On either side I could see the smiling faces of the people who had come to our wedding. And yet, the one face I would have given anything in the world to see was missing— my father's face. At that moment I felt the loss keenly. When he had died two years before, I lost the person I had loved most in the world.

We stepped outside the little chapel into the busy New York street. People walking in Washington Square Park stopped to gawk at us as we came down the steps, but I barely saw them. As we stood waiting for the limousine, an elderly gentleman—

a total stranger—well-dressed and gently smiling, stepped out of the crowd to shake my hand.

"My child," he said, "I know God is going to bless you."

He and I looked at each other for what seemed a long time. He squeezed my hand, tipped his hat and walked away.

I turned to my husband and felt a wave of love and hope wash over me. Yes, God had blessed me twice over. Not only did I have a wonderful husband, but He had also sent me one of His messengers—an angel in a pin-striped suit and a bowler hat—just when I needed him.

—*Cecelia Reed*

J. Bishop Comes Home

I grew up in rural New Hampshire, eldest daughter in a family of six children. In our chaotic household I found refuge in make-believe, often pretending that I was a beautiful girl named "Joan Bishop" (*Joan* from Joan of Arc and *Bishop* from the English translation of my French last name). I never told anyone else about Joan Bishop. It was a secret between God and me.

Little girls grow up, though, and the day came when I bade good-bye to Joan Bishop . . . and to God. I moved to New York, got caught up in a fiercely competitive line of work and gradually found my personal life getting lonelier and lonelier. In time I knew I wanted to return to God, but I hesitated. Would He welcome me back?

One Sunday morning I could not stay away any longer. I went to Grace Church nearby. I walked down the north aisle, past the old pews, each with its own waist-high door and tiny brass nameplates, relics from the last century when parishioners purchased their seats. I chose an empty pew and closed the door behind me.

"Please, God," I began to pray, "I'm lonely and afraid. Are You here? Is this the place for me? Will these people all around me take me in?" I wanted God's assurance that I should stay in that church, but no assurance seemed to come. Suddenly I felt an overpowering urge to leave.

Hastily gathering up my coat and scarf, I opened the pew door and stepped into the aisle. As I turned to shut the old door, my eyes were drawn to its tiny brass nameplate. The plate read: J. BISHOP.

I returned to my seat. I was home again.

—Irma Levesque

The Writing on the Wall

I lay awake nights wondering if we had made the right decision. Our small suburban home would soon be sold, and we would move into a large two-story house in mid-town Memphis. Built in 1914, the fine old home had fallen into disrepair. Faded wallpaper hung in strips from the walls and ceiling. The exposed plaster walls were badly cracked. Nevertheless, my husband and I fell in love with the house with its high ceilings, stained-glass windows and oak moldings.

As moving day drew near, however, my doubts grew. Maybe we had decided too quickly that we could do the restoration work. What if it proved more expensive than we'd expected? I hoped and prayed we had made the right decision. But I was uneasy.

Moving day came and went. Nights and weekends were devoted to stripping wallpaper, replastering walls, stripping paint.

Then one Saturday afternoon I came home to find David stripping the last layer of wallpaper in the dining room. "Debby!" he called excitedly. "Come look." I went over to the wall he had just laid bare. "Here." He pointed to some writing scrawled on it.

There was a name—a workman who had originally plastered the walls? We had no way of knowing.

And there was a date: Nov. 4–14.

The name written on that wall was ours: Bledsoe.

And the date, November 4. That is my birth date.

We were home.

—Debby Ellis Bledsoe

God Does Not Answer Every Prayer

God does not answer every prayer,
Quite aware
How many things we ask in vain
Would pain.

—Edward Lodge Curran

On a Gray and Rainy Day

Five years ago I would have said that my marriage to Jerry was beyond repair. We'd been together for eight years, had two children, and we fought constantly on every conceivable subject, from where to live to what kind of toothpaste to buy. Talking things over had not helped. Neither had marriage counseling. Finally we decided that the only course for us was to get a divorce.

Then Jerry quit his job in New York City because of the long commute, which he hated. We agreed to stay together until he found work closer to home. The months went by, and despite constant effort, he still wasn't able to land a job. Our savings dwindled. First thing I knew we were trapped, forced to live together, and that only heightened the anger. By now we were even sleeping in separate rooms.

I was so upset, so on edge, that I was ready to try anything that might help. One of the things I did was to start attending a weekly prayer service at an Episcopal church not too far away in Darien, Connecticut. It was really a desperation move on my part. From time to time I even suggested to Jerry that he might try a little religion for a change—you can imagine the kind of response *that* got!

And, as a matter of fact, it didn't do me much good, either. The people at that church seemed so alive and in tune with themselves that they only made me feel worse. I felt small, inferior. *But those are the kinds of people that God helps,* I thought, *not some bitter failure like me.*

One night, as a cold December wind blasted the house

outside, Jerry and I sat in the living room having another of
our rasping fights, this one so loud that I was afraid it might
wake little Michael and Greg. Then Jerry left the room and
wham—the bedroom door slammed shut. This was Jerry's way
of telling me that the living room was now my territory. We
had an arrangement that the first person in the bedroom slept
there; the other got the sofa.

Then I heard him snap the lock. "Jerry," I said, banging on
the door, "I need to get my nightgown and robe."

"Sleep without them," he yelled back.

"Open this door!" I screamed.

"Go away," he said.

"Jerry, if you don't open this door now, I *will* go away. I'll
leave you. I'll take the children with me."

There was no answer. I yanked open the linen closet, ripped
out a blanket and a pillow, and stretched out on the sofa fully
dressed. In the darkness, I could hear my heart thumping. *I
said I would leave Jerry—and I will!*

"But, God," I whispered into the night in a kind of prayer,
"where will I go?" Then it became a real prayer. "Please,
God, just this once, help me."

I awakened the next morning to a gray light. A steady rain
drummed on the roof. Jerry and the children were still sleeping. Pulling a coat over my wrinkled clothes, I slipped out the
front door and dashed through the downpour to the car. For
a while I sat on the cold, plastic seat, listening to the noise of
rain on metal. Where *could* I go? I didn't have enough money
even to rent a room. Maybe if I just drove around, my head
would clear and I could think of something.

I drove slowly about our winding country roads. I gripped
the steering wheel hard and squinted my eyes at the blinding
rain on the windshield. Other cars splashed by. I drove on.

A sign ahead said, "Darien." *Yes, Darien,* I thought to myself, *the Tuesday prayer services.* Then it came to me: *Yesterday
was Monday; today is Tuesday.* I looked at my watch. Nine-
thirty. *How odd, the group is just gathering.*

I was a little late when I slipped into the sanctuary of St.
Paul's Episcopal. Slinking down a side aisle, I already felt sorry
that I'd come. In my wet and wrinkled clothes, I was horribly
out of place. More so than usual.

The rector entered the pulpit. Father Terry Fullam. I'd heard him speak before, but I'd never met him. His text, he said, was John 14. He spoke with vigor, animatedly, about the Holy Spirit: "I will pray the Father, and he shall give you another Comforter." All the while I slumped farther down into the pew, feeling so unworthy, so very uncomforted.

Father Fullam stopped abruptly. There was a stirring among the worshipers as he interrupted himself.

"The Lord is moving here," he said. "He has a message for someone in the congregation . . . a woman . . . her marriage is breaking up . . . He wants to heal the relationship."

His words made me shiver. What a coincidence . . .

"For years this woman has been trying to mold her husband into what she thinks he should be. My dear people, if we only realized how our spouses are so busy putting up defenses against us. What we need to do is let go and let God have full rein to do His work."

I couldn't believe it. Could God really be speaking to me? I looked around. Heads were bowed, people were praying for this woman Father Fullam was talking about.

". . . The Lord wants you to give your husband, and yourself, to Him . . ."

Now I knew those words were for me. I was stunned, but fantastically alert; and as the congregation continued to pray, I gradually became aware of a Presence next to me, a Person. I couldn't see Him, I just knew He was there, and He touched me. I felt warmed. His touch seemed to drain me of anger, of bitterness, of self-loathing. I felt as if I were being lifted up, high up, and wrapped tenderly in intricate finery. I felt like a King's child. I *was* a King's child! "Jesus," I whispered.

I gave myself to Him.

After the service, I crossed the parking lot to the car. It had stopped raining and the sky was a hazy quilt of gray and white. The wet tree bark had an ebony shine, and the winter ground was beaded with sparkling drops. Beautiful. The world was beautiful.

I headed the car for home. What would it be like entering the house now—back to the same old anger? But Jesus had said He wanted to heal the relationship. He would heal it, I knew that, but how?

When I pulled into the driveway, there, through the window, I saw Jerry. Swallowing hard, I walked to the door and opened it. His back was to me. "Hello, Jerry," I said quietly. There were no where-have-you-beens, no remonstrations, just a curious kind of look that I'd never seen on his face before.

I hung my coat in the closet and went to the kitchen to prepare lunch. I recalled what Father Fullam had said earlier. "For years this woman has been trying to mold her husband into what she thinks he should be." But Jerry *did* have his fine qualities: his gentle way with the children, his quiet sense of humor that I used to enjoy. Suddenly I wanted to make the best lunch I possibly could. I wanted to make it for Jerry.

Shyly, little Greg tugged at me. "Mommy," he said, "you're singing." I wasn't really, I was humming. I think he'd never heard me hum before.

The four of us ate lunch in near silence. The children seemed to sense that it was a time to be quiet. Jerry kept glancing at me, shyly. I wanted to tell him what had happened, but as it turned out, it was he who had something to tell me.

"A funny thing happened to me this morning. You were gone, and I was sitting here with the kids, and at about 10:30 I had to get up. Something told me that I had to go and find a Bible."

I held my breath.

"Yes, I know," he went on, "it sounds crazy, especially coming from me, but the fact is, I *had* to find a Bible."

I stared at him in amazement.

"It took me a long time until I found where you had left your Bible, but I found it and I opened it and started reading. I read all of the fourteenth chapter of John, about the Holy Spirit helping us."

When I told him what had happened to me, the two of us sat there in disbelief—overwhelmed, afraid, awed, elated, hopeful. Then we found that without realizing it we had reached across the table and were holding hands.

That was the beginning. Today the marriage that I thought was beyond repair is stronger than ever. We had to work at it, of course. I had to find out how to stop nagging and trying to run Jerry; each of us had to learn forbearance and patience and how to appreciate each other's finer qualities. But it was the Lord who made the healing possible, undeserving as we may have been. On a gray and rainy day He simply reached out and touched us with His radiant light.

—*Blenda Connors*

A Home for Irene

I work for a large community hospital in Connecticut, placing patients in nursing homes. Of all my patients, the most difficult to place was Irene Manion.*

No one from any social welfare agency knew her. No one from a church claimed her. She had no relatives, no visitors and apparently no friends. And she required a great deal of medical care.

For months I made hundreds of phone calls to nursing homes, trying to get her admitted. No one would accept her. I became obsessed with finding Irene a home. As I prayed to God each morning before work, I mentioned Irene Manion's name.

One day after an arrangement that had looked hopeful fell through, I just sat at my desk and cried. Staring at Irene's fat, worn, faded paperwork, I said, "God, I give You Irene. Please place her where she'll get the best of care." I was really giving up.

But a few minutes later I was back, dialing a nursing home I had called many, many times before. The admissions person wasn't there, and then, before I knew it, the operator connected me to a hallway wall phone. An evening nurse answered. In my frustration, I told her about my problem.

"What is the patient's name?" the nurse asked. "Irene Manion," I told her, and to my amazement the nurse said, "Send her to us in the morning. I'll arrange everything. She'll get the best of care."

Then the nurse told me how, when her mother had died, she'd been raised by a neighbor, a woman she called "Mom."

*Name has been changed.

Now after twelve years of looking desperately for that woman, her search had ended.

Irene Manion was her beloved "Mom."

—*Mary Anne Hulford*

The Pool in the Desert

My husband was gravely ill. In desperation his doctors prescribed bypass heart surgery, a new and untested procedure at the time. Bob and I were both frightened and needed a reprieve. A week before surgery we packed a picnic and on a glorious California day drove out to the Mojave Desert.

Bob loved the desert air, it was so dry and easy to breathe. We traveled aimlessly on back roads lined with desert flowers, yucca and the lovely paloverde tree. And then, on an off-road track, we chanced upon a path. We left the car, and the path led us to a gentle stream of water. Such streams aren't unheard-of in the Mojave in June, but they're rare.

We sat beside a shaded pool. During the next few hours—picnicking, sunning—we were as happy as we'd ever been during our twenty-five years of marriage. The water—so unexpected, so soothing as we soaked our feet—especially pleased Bob. "The Lord leadeth us beside the still waters," he said to me. And indeed, as we talked, the waters seemed to wash away our fears. Our souls were restored.

Reluctantly we left. But back at the car Bob realized he'd left his knife on a poolside stone and I walked back to retrieve it. There was the knife, glinting in the sun. But the brook . . . the pool . . . they were gone. Where there had been water minutes earlier, there were now only stones and sand.

The following week Bob died on the operating table, his heart condition even worse than the doctors had suspected. I'm sure, though, that he died in peace, assured by our stream that he would dwell in the house of the Lord forever.

—*Betsy Young*

GOD
PROVIDES_____

Thou openest thine hand, and satisfiest the desire of every living thing.

—Psalm 145:16

In one sense the whole Bible is a demonstration of God's care for us in providing for our needs. When God so dramatically provided a sacrifice for Abraham on Mount Horeb, Abraham gave God a new name—The Lord Will Provide—*Jehovah-Jireh.*

Today God is still in the providing business, as these stories show. When we tell Him what we need and ask for His help, He hears and answers. No need is too unimportant to bring to Him—whether detergent for dirty diapers or the maintenance of a balky washing machine. And none is beyond his power—rain in drought, shade for newly planted crops, or money to pay for a Bible.

Sometimes God's answers come with a bit of humor. (How nice to know that we are made in His image.) They also show that when we ask specifically, we get specific answers. Yet sometimes when we don't say what we are specifically asking for, God answers our underlying request. That happened to Abraham when he was concerned for his nephew Lot in Sodom. He never came out and asked God directly to save Lot—yet God answered Abraham's real concern by taking Lot and his family out of the doomed city before it was obliterated.

We can never pin down the exact way God will work, but, always, His gifts show us His love. They do not merely indulge us, but help us along the paths of righteousness, encouraging our eager desire to honor Him and do His will.

As these stories demonstrate, God provides for all our needs—physical, material, emotional, spiritual. And His loving provisions accompany us throughout our lives—from the cradle to the grave. As the Psalmist wrote: "Surely goodness and mercy shall follow me all the days of my life" (Psalm 23:6).

The Unexpected Nickel

On my library shelves are expensive editions of the Bible printed on gold-edged India paper. I have Bibles complete with concordance, interpreter's notes and historical maps. But none mean as much to me as a battered little New Testament I once bought for a nickel.

I can still remember that day: I was about eleven and, after school, rushed with the other boys and girls to our church where one of Billy Sunday's staff was holding a revival service. At the end of the meeting the speaker offered each child a copy of the New Testament for five cents, saying, "In order that you may fix in your hearts the love of God, you should keep with you a portion of the Word of God. I would give it to you free except that yours will mean more to you if you have to give up something for it."

I got up and left the building disconsolately as the boys and girls crowded about to buy their New Testaments. Few things in my life since then have been so keenly desired as that New Testament. But I had no money.

I walked along with my head down, thinking. I was about halfway home when I noticed something shining in the grass. I poked at the strange object with my toe. Excitement took hold of me. I had found a nickel! No, I suddenly knew, God had given me that nickel!

Was it too late? Was the preacher still in church? I had never run faster. Up the street, into the church—yes, he was still there. Breathlessly, I held out my nickel.

"Oh, I'm sorry, they're all gone." Then, seeing my disappointment, he added, "But give me your nickel and your name and address and I'll mail a New Testament to you."

I haunted the postman until my small package arrived. That was my first copy of God's Word, and it introduced me to the riches of the Bible. Who can say how much that New Testament had to do with directing my life in Christian channels?

Others have their one sure proof of God's personal interest in them. I have mine—*God* gave me that nickel!

—*Glenn Asquith*

310 Montgomery Street

When I was eleven years old in Memphis, Tennessee, I prayed and prayed that God would direct my father to buy the bigger house that he and my mother had been considering for their growing family. This house of my dreams was located at 310 Montgomery Street in Memphis.

Silently I rebelled at the possibility that my father might decide instead to move our family to a small town in Mississippi—Starkville—where he had an opportunity to lease and run a hotel. My roots were down deep in Memphis, so I asked God over and over that we might live at 310 Montgomery Street.

However, my father soon announced that he had decided to move our family to Mississippi. Once there, we lived in the hotel. I was very depressed, and when my father told us that he had found a suitable house for the family, I was only mildly interested. I did agree, though, to go with the family to see it.

As we started off in the car, I paid little attention—until I read the street sign as we drove into the block where the house was situated. Then as we parked in front of a pleasant-looking house, I read the numerals over the door . . . and caught my breath.

Here, 130 miles from Memphis, I found that God had answered my fervent prayer with startling exactness and, I'm sure, a twinkle in His eye.

The house my father had chosen for us in Starkville was located at 310 Montgomery Street!

—*Mary Catherine Wallace*

"Trust Me, Tom"

It was probably the gloomiest birthday of all my twenty-three years.

Heat waves shimmered from sidewalks as I trudged along downtown streets in Washington, D.C. Two five-dollar bills curled limp and soggy in my pocket.

Ten dollars to buy my birthday present. I felt a twinge of guilt. Perhaps I shouldn't be spending this with a two-thousand-dollar debt over my head. But then, what difference could such a meager purchase make?

My mother had given me five dollars, and I had hoarded the other bill for this occasion; there would be no other celebration.

Things were tight at home where I lived while attending seminary. Dad had died unexpectedly a little over a year ago, and my mother, three younger brothers and I were barely making ends meet. God, it seemed, had forgotten not only my birthday but everything else about me these days.

"It's your own fault, Tom," an acquaintance gibed. "If you had gone on to teaching high school as you planned, you'd be living in your own apartment by now!"

He was right. I had received a two-thousand-dollar undergraduate scholarship at the University of Maryland on the condition that I would teach in the public schools for at least two years, or repay the state the money.

However, early in undergraduate school, the Lord made it clear that He wanted me to become a missionary. At first I resisted. But in various ways He spoke to my heart again and again. By graduation time I had to make a decision.

On one hand, common sense argued that I go ahead and teach social studies to high school students for two years. Then the debt would be satisfied and I could go on to seminary.

On the other hand, it seemed imperative that I enter seminary right away. I prayed long and hard, seeking direction in the Bible. Proverbs 3:5–6 spoke to me: "Trust in the Lord with all thine heart; and lean not unto thine own understanding. In all thy ways acknowledge him, and he shall direct thy paths."

I decided to trust in Him and entered seminary. As the verse said, "He shall direct thy paths," and to me that meant He would help me work things out.

However, it didn't seem to be panning out that way. Attending seminary in Washington, D.C., was expensive. Even working at the Library of Congress in my free hours barely kept my head above water.

I had to pay that money back to the state of Maryland

shortly, and I had absolutely nowhere to get it. When my brother Brad asked what I was going to do, I could only quote him Proverbs 3:5–6. He shook his head. "Nice words, Tom, but they don't add up to two thousand dollars."

Now as I walked the hot streets of Washington, I speculated as to whether he was right. There was a fine line between faith and recklessness, and I wondered if I hadn't stepped across it.

I even felt uneasy about taking this hour to come downtown with final exams pushing me. But for some strange reason I had felt strongly led to do it. Besides, I knew my mother would be hurt if I didn't get something with the money she had given me. "We'll wait dinner for you," she had said cheerily as I left the house.

Traffic blared on the street and people crowded by as I wandered on. Then I saw it—a shop selling used books.

I peered through the grimy window. In the dim interior were stacked myriads of paperbacks, magazines and thousands of books, shoehorned into hundreds of sagging shelves. It was a sight no young seminarian could resist.

The door creaked open and I stepped into an atmosphere strong with the musty aroma of aged paper and old leather. I discovered that the general disorder was at least divided into departments. One entire corner was labeled "Religion."

Wooden floorboards groaned under my feet as I headed to it. As I browsed the shadowed shelves, it was difficult to read the titles. *Oh, to be able to buy histories and Bible commentaries in mint condition,* I sighed.

Then some ancient leather-bound volumes on a lower shelf caught my eye. Squatting down, I pulled one out and gingerly opened it to the title page. I held in my hands *Job to Solomon's Song, Adam Clarke's Commentary, designed as a help to a better understanding of the Sacred Writings.* I withdrew another: *The Practical Observation of Rev. Thomas Scott, D.D., with extensive Explanatory, Critical and Philological Notes.* The type had been set in Brattleboro, Vermont, in 1836.

I tucked the two books under my arm and reached for more. There was a Wesley's *Commentary* and then two others, five different commentaries in all—each a remnant from some broken set.

I felt I could use them in my seminary studies. The price

seemed a bit steep at two dollars per volume, but I stacked the
lot under my chin and paid at the checkout counter.

Two hours later the finds nestled in my bedroom bookcase.
Downstairs I sat down to dinner with Mom and two of my
brothers. The third was missing.

"Brad," Mom called, "dinner is ready!"

In a minute he bounded excitedly down the stairs.

"Tom," he said, waving a yellowed newspaper clipping,
"you may really have something there."

"Have something where?"

"In those old books you just bought." He thrust the clipping into my hand. "I found this," he announced, "stuck in
among the pages."

I frowned at the fragile newsprint. Then, my dinner completely forgotten, I reread it closely. The long-ago reporter
claimed that the bound proof sheets to Wesley's *Commentary on
the New Testament* had disappeared—lost or stolen—half a century before from a university library in his city. The volume,
he wrote, could be distinguished from the first edition by
numerous word changes by the author, John Wesley, in his
own hand. The reporter went on to list some of the changes.

I rose from the table, my heart pounding. A Wesley's *Commentary* had been in my stack!

I rushed up the stairs, my brother clattering after me. Any
doubts I might have had melted away as we turned the pages.
The changes were all there. And handwritten notes between
author and printer, now brown with age, crowded the mar-
gins. I stared in awe at the original handwriting of John Wesley! Perhaps his brother Charles had quilled a few lines, too.

Changes, some even doctrinal, were discussed at length by
the historic spiritual leader. Barring fraud, I had in my hand
the proof sheets to perhaps the major foundation document of
Methodism!

The next morning I rented the only safety deposit box I had
ever owned. As I enclosed the fragile news clipping with it, I
wondered who had put it in the book. Was it the person who
had originally taken or found the volume and wanted to establish some sort of authenticity? Whatever, after all these years
no one would ever know.

The task ahead now was to establish legal claim to the document, prove authenticity, and get an appraisal. I wasn't quite sure how to begin, but a phone call to the university library from which it had disappeared seemed in order.

The people there thought that it was probably one and the same book. They also assured me that it was mine. All they asked was the name of the bookstore to help them in tracking down and repurchasing other missing materials.

I then went to the public library and was directed to a man who stated that the book wasn't rare. However, he said, if I wished, they would take it off my hands for twenty dollars.

I thought it over and decided to show it to the acquisitions librarian at the Library of Congress where I worked. She suggested that I send it to a New York concern where they appraise and auction off antique books for a twenty percent commission. I followed her advice.

I waited. As months went by, I began wondering if I might have built myself up for a big letdown.

Then a letter arrived from Parke Bernet Galleries in New York City. They had sold Wesley's *Commentary* to the highest bidder for $5,500. Enclosed was a check, minus their commission, for $4,400!

In the nick of time, I had enough money to pay off my undergraduate debt, finance the remainder of my seminary studies and buy a used car.

The car eventually took me on several summer missionary trips to Mexico, where I felt another call to devote full time to its people after graduation. At the border, I worked with teenage drug users, and then became a program director of a missionary radio station, reaching the homes of a million people whose only contact with the outside world is often the little radios that play constantly in their kitchens.

God had not forgotten my birthday that hot day in Washington. His monetary gift has long since been spent on His work. But it served to illuminate a much greater gift: the faith that if I trusted Him despite my own understanding, He would lead me into paths of unbelievable fulfillment that I could never have imagined.

—*Thomas B. Haughey*

The Promise

When the doctor told Dick and me that we could never have a child, we didn't believe it. We went ahead and bought a house on a horseshoe-shaped street where cars didn't go too fast. We chose our yard for the big climbing trees out back, and the neighborhood so that our children wouldn't have to walk far for friends.

But the years passed and no child came. I took to haunting the baby carriages in front of grocery stores and begging my friends to go out so I could baby-sit. Three babies in particular, through the years, I loved in a special way. They were all girls and every one of them had blonde hair and deep green eyes. When I held one of them my heart would start to thump and I'd have to blink back tears.

I couldn't understand it: Neither in Dick's family nor in mine was there yellow hair or green eyes. Yet, each time I picked up one of those babies, I felt that she belonged to me.

And all this while, we prayed—not for a baby, just that His will be done. Yet whenever I pictured His will for us, there was always a baby right in the center of it. I even got the room ready. It wasn't until afterwards that I realized that I'd chosen green walls and yellow curtains.

One warm summer night in 1955, when we had waited seven years without a child, I woke up with a tremendous elation racing through me. I tried to get back to sleep but instead I grew wider awake every minute. At last, afraid that I would wake up Dick, I got up and went into the living room.

I switched on the lamp and sat down in our old brown armchair. On the table beside the chair was a book of Bible quotations. I picked it up but felt too exhilarated to read. It slipped to my lap, falling open. At the top of the page where the book had opened, in letters that looked ten feet tall, were the words: "For with God nothing shall be impossible" (Luke 1:37).

And then the whole living room filled with light. The lamp was on, it's true, but all of a sudden the room was *full* of light—the way sunlight sometimes shines on dust particles, causing one to see that the air all around is crowded and active instead of empty. In the same way I was suddenly aware that Christ occupied the whole room.

After a while the awareness passed, but not the certainty. I never doubted for a moment that Christ had shown me His all-powerful creativity to tell me that our prayers for a child had been answered.

In the morning I told Dick that we were going to have a baby. On the calendar in the kitchen I drew a big red circle around the night before. Then I phoned my mother and told her, and then I told my next-door neighbor. Soon there was scarcely anyone I hadn't told.

"Are you sure?" my mother asked me. "Have you been to the doctor?"

But to me that would have been lack of faith. I had a promise from God! What did I want with a doctor?

But yet as the days passed, doubt arose in my mind too. And at last I didn't need a doctor to be crushingly, utterly certain that no baby was coming to us.

If I had fallen from a mountaintop I couldn't have dropped so far and so hard. I stopped answering the telephone. When my next-door neighbor rapped on the kitchen door I flattened myself against the wall until I heard her footsteps going away. I couldn't see anyone. I couldn't talk about it.

Yet, even at the worst moment of my disappointment, I couldn't get away from what I had seen and felt that night. Something had happened. But what? And how could I have misread it so completely?

That October, more to take my mind off myself than anything else, Dick suggested that we make the rounds of adoption agencies again. We'd been doing this for several years, but the waiting lists were so long that we'd never even gotten our names down. This time, however, one place in New York City was more encouraging. Yes, they would take our application. Yes, we would be hearing from them.

It was in April, the following spring, when a phone call

came. "Mrs. Larsen," the caseworker's voice said, "your little girl is here."

Dick rushed from his office and met me at the adoption agency. We scarcely dared to look at each other. Then the caseworker brought in a small bundle wrapped in a pink blanket. "Here she is," she said.

But I could have picked her out of a thousand babies! There was the little wisp of fair hair, and the green, green eyes.

When Claudia was three weeks old, we brought her back to the green-and-yellow room that had waited for her for so long, back to the house that she had suddenly made a home. With her came a very brief sheet of facts: parents' blood types, length of pregnancy, weight at birth, first formula . . .

All during those busy first weeks I kept trying to put that sheet of paper away, but something wouldn't let me. Like a fly buzzing around my head, something about it wouldn't let me alone. I'd brush it away; a few days later it would be back. The paper. Look at the paper.

At last to quiet the buzzing once and for all, I picked it up from the kitchen table where it had lain and began to read. My eyes stopped at the space for the months and weeks before the date of birth. It was very precise, down to the number of days. Slowly I took down the calendar from the wall and, getting last year's calendar from a drawer, I began counting back.

I knew the answer before I ever got to the month with the triumphant red circle. But I finished the count. And with the last number my finger rested on the very day and night when our house had filled with the promise.

We were indeed to have a baby, that much I had grasped. That another was to bring her into the world, I had not guessed. Nor did I know what confusion and grief were the other part of the story, nor how in His love Christ was reaching out at that moment to the boy and girl who were the parents. I only know that in His mercy He reached out to us, too, and that the new little life so marvelously beginning was ours from the very moment of conception.

"Bone of my bones and flesh of my flesh" (Genesis 2:23) are lovely words, the loveliest—I used to think—that a mother could say. But I know more beautiful ones still, the words I

say to my daughter: "Hope of my hope, longing of my heart,
the promise of my Lord."

—*Fran Larsen*

To an Adopted Child

Not flesh of my flesh,
Nor bone of my bone,
But still miraculously my own.
Never forget
For a single minute
You didn't grow under my heart,
But in it.

—*Fleur Conkling Heyliger*

Out of Detergent

Two months after my husband finished graduate school and
started a new job, I gave birth to our first child. We had very
little money and at times we had none at all.

The days went by and I eked out this and eked out that.
Then one morning after I'd gathered up the baby's laundry,
I found I'd run out of detergent. Our monthly paycheck wasn't
due till the end of the week, and we barely had enough money
left for our food needs, never mind soap. But I *had* to have
clean diapers for my baby! It was one of those little frustrations
that wells up to blimp-size discouragement.

"O Lord, You know I need soap. I pray that my folks send
me money—soon." My parents periodically sent a small check.
They were the only source I could think of.

I heard a noise at the door. Could it be the mail carrier?
Somehow I actually expected God would answer me that
quickly. I glanced out the window, but no mailman. It must
have been the wind rattling the screen.

I went on with my housework. I kept crying out to the Lord. "What will I do about these diapers? O Lord, what will I do?"

Then suddenly I felt prompted to go to the front door. Perhaps the carrier *had* come and I'd missed seeing him. Perhaps a check . . .

I opened the door and hanging on the handle was a plastic sack containing a sample box of a new detergent!

What did I learn about prayer that day? That God not only answers prayers but also has His own way of chiding a too-frantic housewife. Isaiah 65:24 (TLB) says, "While they are still talking to me about their needs, I will go ahead and answer their prayers!"

—*Shirley Pope Waite*

The Machine That Didn't Act Up

In 1968 my husband, Billy, was about to go to Vietnam, leaving me in Nashville with a three-year-old, a second child on the way—and an erratic old washing machine. Every morning the machine would merely complete its wash cycle and then stop dead, its tub full of soapy undrained water. Billy had a way of fixing the machine: taking the top off, jiggling a wire. But what would we do when Billy went away? In the meantime I prayed for Billy's safe return to us, and I didn't think about the washing machine until the day after he left.

That morning I reluctantly filled the machine with dirty clothes and then said, "Lord, what am I going to do with a three-year-old, a new baby and a busted washer? Please, God, help me through this."

An hour later I returned to the machine and—to my amazement—the clothes had gone through a complete wash and rinse, and were now ready for the dryer! For days after that the washer continued to work perfectly. Soon I forgot the problem altogether.

In January 1969 Billy came safely home. He brought a duffel bag of dirty clothes. That very day I threw them into the machine and quickly returned to the living room to be with Billy as he got to know our new son.

An hour later I went back to the washing machine. Can you guess what I found?

Soapy undrained water!

I could only laugh and feel more blessed than ever. Billy was home and the washer was back to its old dirty tricks!

—Annette Sims

Call for Help

Two days before Christmas, while a sleet storm beat against the windows, I was alone in the house with my sick baby. By mid-afternoon her temperature had flared to 104 degrees, and my hand shook, holding the thermometer. The year before, despite all medical science could do, our little boy had died of pneumonia. Ellen had to have a doctor right away.

But how? I was without a car. My husband, a flood engineer in the Tacoma office, had put our car in the shop for new brake linings before he left for three days to measure the rising water of the Skagit River. And with no telephone (we'd moved into this new house only last week and ours wasn't yet installed), I'd have to run across the street to the one house besides ours here on this hilltop and ask to use theirs to call a doctor.

Bending over the baby's crib, which I'd pulled into the living room where it was warmer, I listened to her quick shallow breathing.

"Darling, Mommy's going to get help for you!" Snatching up raincoat and scarf, I hurried out the door.

Yesterday, a warm chinook wind had partially melted our recent snowfall. Today, freezing temperatures formed icicles along the dripping eaves and coated trees and telephone wires with ice.

Frozen ridges of snow crackled beneath my feet as I ran across to my neighbors', praying they were home. On their front porch I rang the doorbell once, and after a few seconds, again, long and hard. No one came. Then I recalled hearing their car go out early in the morning. If they were away for the entire holiday weekend, what was I going to do? Shivering, I looked down our long, unpaved hill leading to the nearest built-up area, twelve or more blocks away. If only some car would drive up here now! Anyone would be glad to call a doctor for me. Our hilly street ended in a cul-de-sac, so we had little traffic aside from an occasional delivery truck or the postman—who had already come earlier in the day. Of course, I could phone from one of the houses along the bus line, but I was afraid to leave Ellen while I went down there and back. Would I dare bundle her up and take her with me in this freezing weather?

As I started back across the street, with sleet stinging my cheeks and wind tearing at my scarf, I slipped and fell, wrenching my ankle—not badly, only enough to warn me that carrying the baby down our slippery hill would be dangerous. There had to be some way to reach a doctor! And suddenly I knew what I was going to do.

I turned and went back onto my neighbors' porch where I rang the bell again, just to be certain. My heart thumping, I tried the knob. *Would this be "breaking and entering"?*

The door didn't open; it was locked. But sometimes people leave a key beneath the mat. I lifted the mat. No key. So down the steps once more and around to the back porch. I was going to get to that telephone if I had to break a window! Luck, however, was with me. Beneath a flowerpot I found the key, unlocked the door and tiptoed into a strange kitchen, half-expecting someone to leap out at me crying, "What are you doing here?"

But the house was silent, and there on a little stand in the hall stood the blessed telephone! No directory to find a doctor's phone number, so I dialed the operator. A buzzing and crackling sounded and an indistinct voice said something.

"Operator?" I called. "This is an emergency. I am alone with a very sick baby. I must have a doctor."

The faraway voice answered, but I couldn't understand a single word. I gave my address and repeated my request, "Please send me a doctor!"

Then came an explosive noise and the line went dead. The wires, probably heavy with ice, had broken down. Did my call

for help get through? Had someone heard? There was no way
of knowing.

When I opened our door, Ellen was crying—the pitiful wail
of a sick baby. After I'd sponged her hot little body, I sat in
the rocking chair, coaxing her to take her bottle with a quarter
tablet of aspirin dissolved in orange juice. I knew nothing else
to do. If only Jim were here, he'd find a doctor. His office
could reach him, send for him to come home. But how could
I call the office without a phone? I thought of my mother and
father and my younger sister and brother getting ready for
Christmas in Portland.

"We're only across the Columbia River from you!" Dad
always said. Now they seemed a thousand miles away.

Suddenly I heard the sound of a car engine laboring up our
icy hill. Quickly I put Ellen back into her crib and ran bare-
headed out the door. But the car had lost traction and stalled,
and already the driver was backing down, too concerned with
his steering and too far away to notice my signals.

I went slowly back into the house. My mind felt numb. I
couldn't seem to think. I tried to get the latest weather report
of the storm, but now the radio was dead. Down in the basement, I put more wood in the furnace. Then I brewed a fresh
pot of coffee in the kitchen, thankful that neither the furnace
nor the gas range were dependent upon electricity. The pungent odor of coffee reminded me I had eaten nothing all day,
so I made oven-toast and sat with it and my coffee mug, staring
at the little Christmas tree Jim had brought home before he
left. "Fresh off the slopes of Mount Rainier," he'd told me. Its
crisp branches were festooned with strings of electric lights,
ready to be lit for Ellen's first Christmas. We'd hoped that
watching her joy would help to soften the memory of our grief
a year ago. Now she was too sick to notice the silver birds and
shining balls.

When December's early dusk closed in, since the electricity
was off I searched out candles and watched their flames flutter
in the icy air seeping beneath the windowsill. From time to
time I glanced across the street, hoping to see lights in my
neighbors' windows. But they remained dark.

When Ellen awoke crying, I took her up and, huddling in
the big morris chair, held her against my shoulder, bracing

myself to endure the long hours ahead until Jim got home. What did the pioneer mothers do in the olden days when their children were sick and no doctor was nearer than a hundred miles away? Then I seemed to hear my grandmother's voice answering me: "Why, we prayed."

So with my cheek against my baby's silken head I *tried* to remember some prayer, but the words wouldn't come. I was so tired and discouraged, and God seemed far away. But I think *all of me* must have gone out in a silent cry for help, for as Ellen quieted and I leaned back in the chair, breathing the spicy fragrance of the Christmas tree and staring at the candles' flickering light, gradually fear and tenseness began to drain away. A feeling of peace and comfort closed about me.

I woke with a start, knowing someone had entered the room. Hadn't I locked the door? In the candlelight, a tall man stood looking down at me.

"I am the doctor," he said.

Afterward, I could never remember his face—only the kindness and compassion in his voice. When he examined the baby, she scarcely stirred beneath his gentle hands.

"No lung congestion. But her ears are infected. This medication will help. Keep her warm—let her sleep—she'll be much better by this time tomorrow. Stop worrying, Mother! Try to get some rest." Then he was gone.

For the rest of the night I dozed in the morris chair beside Ellen's crib. She slept straight through fourteen hours! By the time Jim got home on Christmas Eve, her temperature was normal. She was ready to smile at her daddy, and point at the unlighted Christmas tree, saying, "See? Pitty!"

Knowing she would be all right was our most precious Christmas gift.

Days later, after the ice storm was over and its damage repaired, Jim went to the telephone company to try to locate the doctor who had come at midnight. "I want to pay his bill," Jim said. But, of course, the company had no record of my call.

When I went across the street to apologize for my "breaking and entering," the neighbors offered their explanation: "The telephone wires were so mixed up," they said. "Maybe when you thought you were talking to an operator, you were really connected with a hospital that took your message.

Well, maybe . . .

We never found out about our midnight doctor—who he was or how he came. But I believe that after I'd done everything I knew to do for the baby, a Higher Power had heard my silent prayer and sent me help. And sometimes I think of that passage in the Bible, Hebrews 13:2: "Be not forgetful to entertain strangers: for thereby some have entertained angels unawares."

—Dorothy Rood Stewart

God Answers Prayer

I know not when He sends the word
That tells me fervent prayer is heard;
I know it cometh soon or late,
My part is but to pray and wait.
I know not if the blessing sought
Will come in just the guise I thought.
I leave all care with Him above,
Whose will is always one of love.

—Author Unknown

105 Chairs

Just six of us, with me as pastor, were trying to revive a 139-year-old Congregational church. People scoffed. No one had worshiped there for twenty-two years, they said, and besides, it was summer, when even established churches had low attendance. Where would the people come from?

Even so, getting ready for our first service, we set out eighty folding chairs. After we asked God to bless our efforts, Shirley Krohn said, "Remember the Bible story where the poor widow asks the prophet Elisha for help?"

I remembered the story (2 Kings 4:1–7). The widow is in

debt; her only possession is a little pot of oil. Elisha tells her to collect all the empty containers in the village and pour oil into them from her pot. Every vessel is filled. She sells the oil and pays her creditors.

"If the Lord filled all those vessels with oil," said Shirley stoutly, "why can't He fill these eighty chairs with people?"

"Or why can't He fill even more chairs?" someone cried impetuously.

So, after dusty attics and storage sheds were scoured, we had 105 chairs set out, the most that would fit in the room—which left me more apprehensive than ever.

On Sunday the Connecticut weather was perfect for golf and the beach, but at ten o'clock the cars started appearing. In the Bible story, when all the vessels were full, the oil stopped pouring. On this day, when the room filled up, the cars stopped coming. And then the ushers brought me a note: "One hundred and three chairs are filled; the two of us will sit in the two empty seats."

Exactly 105 people for 105 chairs. Yes, God does hear—and answer. Mysteriously. Lovingly. And sometimes, I believe, smilingly.

—George Eckstein

Surprise at Sunrise

From far away came a terrifying noise. As I realized it was the alarm, I groaned. How could it be four o'clock already?

It was Easter morning, and I was in charge of the outdoor sunrise service at our church, Emmanuel Methodist. My long-suffering husband and I bundled our three small sons into the car and drove to the church.

A pantomime of the events between the Last Supper and the resurrection was quite an undertaking, involving a cast of almost thirty teenagers and young adults, and tons of props. Two months of rehearsal were behind us. I was so tired that the back of my neck felt like fire. I knew the others were just as tired.

What if no one came? I wondered as I entered the dark

building. *What if the choir didn't show up? What if—?* I stopped myself. Instead of more doubts, I closed my eyes and whispered for the last time the brief prayer that had been repeated by all of us in the past few weeks.

"Father, just use us. Let the people see *Your* hand in this."

I heard laughter outside, and two teenagers came in, reporting they had forgotten their thongs. Then everyone seemed to come in a rush. I went from group to group, going over their cues.

Somewhere in this confusion we discovered that no one had been asked to supply the sound effects when it came time for the cock to crow. Panic-stricken, I searched out each cast member, begging for someone to imitate a rooster. Under different circumstances, those rooster auditions would have been hilarious. But now they were merely frustrating. The only passable crower in the group was a choir member who would be in full view of the audience.

I sneaked a peep outside. The churchyard was full. An audience like that, and no rooster!

I saw the minister taking his place as narrator. This was his first church, and he was as nervous as I. He motioned for the cast to take its positions. Too late now to find a rooster. The young man who was to portray Christ passed me. He was a new convert, and his face was as white as his robe. I tried to smile, the service started, and the rooster was forgotten.

I watched from behind the church door as the characters began to move silently in accordance with the passage of Scripture being read. Somehow in the first light from the sun, the words took on a new reality. The stillness felt actually holy.

When the boy portraying Peter bent to warm his hands at our small fire, I remembered the rooster. I hoped fervently that the minister would not pause at the passage. The words came clearly:

"And immediately, while he yet spake, the cock crew" (Luke 22:60).

The young minister's rich voice faltered, his hands holding the Bible shook, and even the crowd caught its breath as it happened. Faintly, yet ever so distinctly, from the direction of the city limits, came the crow of a rooster heralding the dawn. Into the silence came the cry—once, twice, three times!

The cast was stunned. The minister recovered and went on. There was no time to speak to one another, but there was an awareness in the air, like electricity. Had God performed a little miracle just for us?

The rest of the service was like a dream. Each actor who came off whispered, "Did you hear the rooster?" As the closing hymn died away, the audience began to buzz, "Did you hear the rooster?"

During the following week the word spread throughout the community. "You should've been at the sunrise service. When the preacher came to the place where the rooster crowed, one did—three times! It was—well—like a miracle."

With all the gigantic problems and needs of our world, this experience may seem trivial. But I wonder—doesn't God work in small as well as big events? I think He does, for exciting things have happened to people in our church. As for me, I have come to look for God's hand in the little things of each day.

—Betty Head

Mandy, Ebenezer & Me

This is a story about a very tiny miracle. And about how, on a summer's day some years ago, a dog, a cat and I headed out into the world together, not knowing where we were going, just trusting that God knew.

The dog's name was Mandy; she was my woolly old English sheep dog. The cat's name was Ebenezer; he was a large gray-and-white tom, and Mandy's beloved companion. As for me, well, I was a not-too-satisfied ex-schoolteacher who had taken early retirement from a school in New Jersey where I had especially enjoyed teaching gifted children. I'd gone to live near my daughter in Rolla, Missouri, but I was restless there. I yearned to be using my special talents for teaching again.

For a while I tried my hand at various local jobs and community activities. I taught in a school for children with dyslexia, I directed the children's choirs at the Presbyterian and Methodist churches, taught rhythms at the local Headstart school, and organized a sing-along group for senior citizens. Still restless, I kept praying for something else to open up.

Eventually I applied for a teaching job in Africa; it had just been filled. I wrote to a small Christian school in Florida; their enrollment, they said, was too uncertain to ask me to come. I tried for a position in a nursery school in Las Vegas; they were sorry, but I was really not qualified.

Then boldly, prayerfully, I made a decision. I would put the little house I'd bought on the market. If God wanted me to do something different with my life, I told myself, the house would sell quickly. If it didn't, then I'd make an effort to relax, and try once more right where I was. The house sold immediately!

One morning I loaded the luggage rack on top of my little foreign sports car, and with Mandy taking over the back seat and Ebenezer and his box on the front seat beside me, my little family and I started out. We drove out to the highway. "All right, God," I said, "we give ourselves over to Your care."

And the three of us just sat there. Which way to go? In my mind I suddenly saw a picture of the Pacific Ocean. Since I'd always wanted to be near the water, we turned and headed west.

The beginning of the journey seemed pleasant enough. Every hour or so I would stop and give Mandy and Ebenezer a little exercise. Mandy was so big that she could barely stand upright or turn around in the car, but she was obviously enjoying the trip. Ebenezer merely endured his box. He didn't really like traveling or being walked on a leash, but Mandy consoled him often by licking his face.

Then after a day or two, trouble. Even in the early dawn the summer heat was stifling. At Cheyenne, the temperature soared to over a hundred degrees. Our car did not have air conditioning and the heat was almost unbearable. Before leaving town I bought a small rug, which I dampened and put in the back for Mandy to lie on. Then we entered a long stretch of desert with few gasoline stations. I could see that we faced many miles before our next stop.

Now in my concern for the animals, I began to worry. Had I been too presumptuous, expecting God to watch over us in this brash journey of mine? For a moment I was inclined to think that I had been in error, in spite of all my prayers. And then my thoughts did a flip-flop. Maybe I hadn't been presumptuous *enough!* All along the way I'd put my trust in God. Why should I stop now?

"O God," I cried out, "I believe in You completely, I do, really do. I know You're there, watching over the three of us." I gripped the hot steering wheel hard. "And please take care of Mandy and Ebenezer. They're so miserable and so hot!"

To explain what happened next is difficult. I can still hardly believe it. On the windshield a few drops of water appeared, and then a few more, until soon the gentlest of rains was falling. I was bewildered. All around us there was broiling sunshine, but immediately over us I could see a cloud just big enough to cover our car. The rain lasted only a few minutes, but it cooled us off. When it stopped, I looked up again. The cloud was still there. And there it stayed, racing along with us as we zipped off the miles while I prayed and Ebenezer purred. When I looked back at Mandy and saw the wind whipping through her shag, I was sure I found her smiling.

So that's all there was to it. God had found a way to prove to us that we were in His care. And in His care we remained, for as you might have guessed, we traveled on with utter confidence and soon landed in the friendly city of Santa Barbara along the Pacific Ocean. There, not surprisingly, I met a group of fine people who were just then starting an organization called "The Friends of the Gifted." In no time I was teaching a class of parents and teachers for the local city college, and Mandy, Ebenezer and I were most content.

Do I really expect you to believe this tale about our little cloud? Yes, I do. Not just because it happened (which it did), but because I think you want to believe it. And wanting to believe—ah, that's the first step to faith itself.

—*Irene Dodson*

What Is Faith?

It is trust beyond all doubting
In God Who rules above!
It is obedience without question.
It is resting in His love.
It is smiling through the teardrops
It is struggling through each test.
It is the firm belief our Father
Is a God Who knoweth best!
It is knowledge He will give us
Light for each step of the way;
Grace for problems we encounter
And strength for each new day.

—Lois Mae Cuhel

The Rain and the Corn

Sometimes, when I get halfway through telling about how
God put His signature on my uncle's corn crop, a few people
get a kind of skeptical look on their faces.

This uncle, Roger H. Geisbert, had a small farm in Freder-
ick County, Maryland. Back in 1964—he was about seventy-
six at the time—a fierce drought killed his hay, barley and
wheat crops. He was desperate to save the corn so he could
feed his little herd of purebred milking shorthorn cattle. The
cornstalks were firing—drying clear up to the tassel—and
when he saw that, Uncle Roger dropped to his knees right
there in the cornfield and asked God to send rain. When he
finished praying, he said, "Now, God, show me You heard my
prayer." Then he got up and walked back toward the house.

Before he even got to the porch, a beautiful freshening rain
was falling—out of a sky that was nearly cloudless—and the
very next day there was a heavy, soaking rain, enough to grain
out the ears of corn. Uncle Roger knelt and thanked God for
answering his prayer.

Coincidence? Maybe. But don't decide till you hear the rest of the story.

Uncle Roger's crop matured very nicely. He tied the bucks, and as the corn ripened, he went to cutting it and then to the shucking. He was nearly finished—and he almost tossed it onto the pile without noticing—when he found the sign from God that he'd requested. It is an object that he later had framed and that I treasure to this day—a beautiful ear of corn, all golden kernels except for the scarlet ones forming a neat and perfect cross.

—*Paul G. Geisbert, Sr.*

The Name on the Mailbox

"Be bold and mighty forces will come to your aid." That's an adage I've long believed in. But there was a moment in my life that has led me to believe that if you're bold, sometimes mysterious forces will come to your aid.

At that time, when my family was struggling, I sought a job with Oklahoma's Department of Human Services. This was a bold move, for I had no diploma, having dropped out of school to marry, but eventually I passed a test and got the job.

My assignment was locating and assisting needy families, and locating them was often difficult. This particular day in 1977, I'd heard of a needy family (no father present, little money or food, frightened mother and children) living near Lake Texoma. This was dangerous country, but I felt it was my duty to find them. I drove all morning with little to guide me, and in this gun-crazy backcountry you didn't just knock on any shack and ask for directions.

Finally, in early afternoon I parked in the shade of a cottonwood and began to pray, asking God to direct me. I then looked down the lane I'd already driven over twice, and there was a lone mailbox plainly emblazoned with the family's name.

My visit went well; we'd be able to help this family with food and clothing. As I was leaving, the grateful mother mar-

veled that I'd found her house. "It wasn't hard," I said, "once
I saw your name on the mailbox."

"My name?" the woman said to me obviously mystified.

And going back to the road, I examined the mailbox again.
There was no name. No name at all.

—*Virginia Cottrell*

Hattie's Garden and How It Grew

I knew how these old people felt. They had worked in gardens
almost all their lives, raising fresh vegetables and greens, but
now they were too old or too sick to grow anything for themselves. Most of them didn't have a place to make a garden
anyway, and they were too poor to buy what they needed at
the store. A lot of them were just going hungry.

Working with a community help program, I would go to
their homes, carrying food to them, and they would say, "Hattie, have you got any vegetables that you can spare?" Or, "Oh,
if you could just bring me a bunch of turnip greens."

I had been a farm worker myself for twenty years and I knew
something about raising crops. But I couldn't see any way to
help these poor people. Farmland is expensive around the
Florida Everglades, and nobody I knew of was going to just
up and hand over a piece of his farm for nothing.

When I would pray I would often mention the problem to
the Lord. "Lord," I said one time, "I don't think I could find
somebody to give even Your angel some land to raise something for free."

Right then a little voice whispered back: "Didn't I say that
if you walk upright, I will give you your heart's desire?"

I wasn't sure that I was hearing anything but my own heart
talking. But it got me thinking.

One day I was driving by the Glades Correctional Institu-
tion, a prison farm near Belle Glade, and I noticed a piece of
black, mucky ground alongside a ditch. It didn't look like it

was being used. So I decided I'd go see the prison farm's superintendent about it.

When I got up to the main building, I just went in and told the man at the desk that I wanted to see the superintendent.

"You have to see him by appointment," he told me.

"Well, just give me an appointment," I said. And believe it or not, he did.

So the day came for the appointment, and I went back out there. I was taken right into the superintendent's office. He seemed like a nice man, and when I told him I'd like to use that patch of land, he said, "What do you want with those thirteen acres?"

I hadn't known it was that much land. "One acre will be enough," I told him. "Even the ditch bank will do. All I want to do is try to raise some fresh food for these old people on fixed incomes, and the ones that can't hoe and make a garden for themselves."

"You mean to tell me *you* want to make a garden?" he said, looking at me like he didn't think an old lady like me could ever do such a thing.

"I want to try," I told him.

"I've got to write the state to get approval," he said. "But if they say it's okay for you to have an acre to work on, it's okay with me, too." I thanked him really sincerely and went out of there rejoicing, but still wondering if it could be so.

Well, I wasn't going to leave it entirely up to the state officials, so I called my praying band together, a little group who get together and tell God what we need. And the band started telling the Lord about that land.

A few weeks later the superintendent called me and said, "I want you to meet with me." So I went out to the prison farm again, and when I went in to see him, the superintendent said, "Mrs. Fields, I got you the whole thirteen acres. The state said okay."

I thought I'd faint. But I gave the superintendent a big smile and said, "Okay, thank you, sir."

Then I began to think of how I was going to work that land. I didn't have a tractor, a hoe or anything else. "I'm going to need a tractor to disk the land with," I told the superintendent.

"Well, that's one thing I can't help you with," he told me.
"The regulations just don't allow for that."

I had the land, but what could I do with it now that I had
it? "O God," I prayed, "help me think."

There is a government assistance program called Manpower
that helps poor people find jobs. So I went over there and
talked to the director. "I'm going to need somebody to help
me grow the old people's garden," I said. "It would be a
chance to help some men help themselves."

I gave the Manpower people the information they wanted,
and the director told me, "We'll see what we can do."

On the morning that we were to get started preparing the
ground, I went out to the prison farm and waited for whom-
ever the Manpower people would send me. Nine men showed
up; I thanked the Lord.

When I told the nine workers what we were going to do,
one of them said to me, "Okay, lady, where's the tractor?"

"O Lord, honey," I said, trying to make them understand
how hard they were going to have to work, "we don't have
a tractor. We only got six hoes." That was all I'd been able to
borrow.

"You think we can make a farm with six hoes?" he said. I
told him, "We're going to try it." I knew the Lord had provided for us so far; I just had to have the faith to believe He
would keep it up.

It was the summertime then, and that old Everglades sun
was beating down on us out there. I wasn't sure anything
would grow in that heat; it just seemed like it would burn up
anything we planted. But we went to work, planting the seeds
that the county had given us.

We beat that ground with our hoes; we dug; we planted. We
beat; we dug; we planted. After a while, something green
started coming up. As it grew more and more, we could see
that it was something we hadn't planted. It was a long, silky-
looking grass that I'd never seen before.

I knew that strange grass would just choke out our little
vegetable plants, if they ever came up. So we started attacking
that grass with our hoes, trying to chop it out. But the more
we fought it, the more it grew. It just kept coming up.

"Lord," I said, "now I'm going to waste all those seeds that

the county gave me. The Manpower people are going to come
out here to see what we're doing with their money, and
they're not going to see a thing but this good-for-nothing
grass. I don't know what else to do, Lord."

Then I went over to the men, standing there with the muddy
hoes in their hands, sweat pouring off their faces in that hot
sun. "We're just going to have to give it up and let the grass
grow," I told them. "Let's just hoe around the ditch bank and
let the people know we're still out here trying to do the garden."

The men were shaking their heads, starting to move over to
the ditch bank. Then I said, "Wait. We ain't done all we can
do. We're going to join hands and we're going to pray."

They looked at me like I was crazy, but they linked their big,
rough hands and we prayed. "Lord," I said, "bless this crop.
We're Your people, Lord. Let the crop come up. Bring it up,
Lord. Bring it on up now."

Well, that grass kept growing. It grew so high, it started to
bend over, and it would blow around in the air, like strands
of silk, the prettiest and strangest grass I had ever seen. And
we kept working around that ditch bank, cleaning out around
there, so we could plant some more, and letting the prison
farm superintendent know we were still out there working.

After about a month, while I was there at the ditch bank with
the men, a voice whispered to me and said, "Why don't you
walk over there and see if that strange grass has died?" I
thought maybe the sun was getting to me, to be hearing voices
like that. But the urge was so strong that I just had to go do
it.

When I started heading that way, the men asked me,
"Where you going?"

"I'm going across the field to look at the strange grass," I
told them.

"For God's sake," one of them said, "don't put us back in
that stuff."

"Just stay where you are," I told them, and I walked on
across the field.

When I got over there, I could see the grass was taller than
ever. But it had bent down like an umbrella over the rows, so
thick you could hardly see down through it. As I walked

through it, I looked down. And there in the rows, shaded by the grass, were the biggest, prettiest turnip greens you ever saw!

The sun was high in the sky, and I wiped the sweat from my face and said to myself, *I knew it was too hot in this sun. I'm seeing what I can't believe I'm seeing.* I wiped my eyes again and looked again. Yes, that's what they were—the prettiest greens I ever saw.

I called out to the men, "Put your hoes down and come running!"

"What do you see?" they yelled back. "A snake?"

"No, I don't see a snake!" I shouted. "Just come running!"

They came jumping and running over. When they got close, I said, "Just look under there," pointing down to the strange grass. They pulled the grass back and saw those big, pretty greens for themselves.

"This ain't ever been in history before that the crop grew under the grass!" one of them said.

"But it's in history now," I said. "You can see it. The Lord has suffered it to be so. He caused it to grow so it could protect our crop for the old people."

Then the men began to rejoice and thank God, and I was praying, "Thank You, Lord! Thank You!"

We began to pull the greens and carry them out to the truck. We started distributing them among the poor, every day. And the more we distributed, the more grew under that grass.

One of the farmers from around Belle Glade saw the turnip and the mustard greens we were carrying to the poor families. "Where are you all getting such pretty greens shipped from this time of year?" he asked me.

"Just come and see," I told him.

When he came out to our garden, he couldn't believe what he saw. "Where did you get this grass to hide your crop?" he wanted to know.

"It came directly from God," I said.

After the Lord gave us such a crop of greens—more than the three hundred poor families we were giving them to could eat—we started planting other vegetables. We planted okra, squash, corn, hot peppers, bell peppers, collard greens, lima beans. And God made it all grow for us. It was just beautiful.

Some families began working special little plots in the thirteen acres. And the nine men kept on gardening the rest, giving the vegetables to the sick and the blind and the other handicapped and old people who couldn't do field work for themselves.

That all happened in 1973, and we have made many a crop since then. But that grass never did come back again.

When I tell people how the Lord did that miracle for the people who would share in our garden, they don't know what to make of my story of how the Lord took care of us. One woman said to me, "Well, that's sure a beautiful philosophy."

"It's not a philosophy," I said. "It's a real thing. God is real. He did it. And you can believe it."

—*Hattie Fields*

Give Me a Strong Heart

Dear Father,
give me a strong heart
that will not wither away
in puny faith.
But may each delay,
each disappointment,
each closed door
be a signal
to hold on more tightly,
to pray more fervently,
to trust more completely,
confident that when the answer comes,
it will be right.

—*Viola Jacobson Berg*

The Gift of Theodora

Several months ago I moved eight hundred miles away from my family to start my first job after college. I loved my work.

But coming home to the emptiness of the apartment I'd rented—that was no fun!

Early one morning I was wakened by what could only be the meowing of a cat—and it was close by. I got up to investigate. In the kitchen, I found the back door open—I was certain I'd locked it the night before—and, to my amazement, there was a tattered, green-eyed tiger cat striding imperiously around the room. Quickly I made a search of the apartment. Nothing was missing; nothing had been tampered with. Reassured, but puzzled, I knelt to pet the cat. She nuzzled against me, purring contentedly.

A few days passed and no one in the neighborhood claimed her and no one advertised for a lost cat. By that time it would have been hard to give her up—we clearly enjoyed each other's company.

"I guess it's safe to name you, my friend," I told her. "I'm going to call you Theodora."

That night, during my weekly phone call home, I told my mother about my new four-footed roommate.

"I'm glad you have a pet, JoLynne!" she said. "I've been worried about you being so lonely. In fact, I've been praying about it every day." And then she chuckled. "Wherever did you get that name—Theodora?

"I don't know, Mom. It just came to me out of nowhere— the way she did."

What neither of us knew then—but I learned later—was the derivation of the name Theodora. It's from the Greek: *Theo,* God; *dora,* gift. Theodora—the cat, like her name, God's gift!

—*JoLynne Walz*

The Yellow Kite

I stood at the window and watched the neighborhood children flying their kites on the hill behind our house. My four-year-old son, Michael, stood next to me with his face eagerly pressed against the glass. Then, looking up at me with pleading eyes, he again asked if he could have a kite like the other children.

For days now, ever since he had first seen them congregate on the hill, Michael had been asking the same question, and had been given the same answer: "Wait until you are a little older."

It was easier not to go into a long explanation, but actually Michael was too young to fly a kite all by himself, and that meant that one of his parents would always have to go with him to help. Because of my health I simply didn't have the strength or energy, and my husband was usually at work. Once again, Michael hid his face in my skirt, something he always did when he was going to cry and didn't want me to see.

As I turned from the window, I felt like crying myself. I looked around the room. The furniture was shabby and worn, and the walls were badly in need of paint. You could see the light places on them, the spots where previous tenants had hung their pictures. Even though we had lived here for several months, I had not done very much to fix the place up. We had moved so many times, and each time it seemed the neighborhood was a little more run-down, and the house a little older, each one in need of repairs.

My husband, Bill, worked long, irregular hours at his job and earned a good salary. However, there was never enough money and we kept going deeper in debt. I had lost three children through miscarriages, and the complications that followed caused me to make several emergency trips to the hospital and to be constantly under a doctor's care. As a result, a tension had grown between us and we found we could no longer get along with one another.

It all looked so hopeless; even God seemed to have forgotten us. I prayed so often about our problems, asking God for help, but things only seemed to get worse. I found myself thinking, *God doesn't care, and I guess I don't either.*

I walked over to the mirror and studied my reflection. It was almost like looking at a stranger. I looked pale and worn, much older than my years. I no longer bothered to fix my face or do anything with my hair. I stepped back and studied my whole image—the old dress that I had worn all week was wrinkled and torn at the pocket, and there was a button missing at the neck.

As I stood there and stared at myself, a feeling of dread,

almost panic, came over me, and it filled my whole body with fear. It was the realization that I was giving up on life. I had stopped caring about anything; I felt defeated. I could no longer rise above the depression that had taken hold of me.

In the last few months, my husband had grown rather quiet and we did not talk much. I was aware of his eyes studying me when he thought I was preoccupied with something. I used to be so particular about everything. Bill had not said a word about the change that had come over me, but his actions said a lot. He made a special effort to get me interested in new things, but I did not respond. In fact, I did not respond to him in any way, and he did not know quite how to handle me anymore.

Michael was the one spark of life left for me. He could make me smile, and when he hugged me, I would feel love. I clung to him much in the way one would cling to a life preserver. He needed me and I knew it—that kept me going.

As I tucked him into bed that evening, Michael said, "Mommy, may I pray to God to send me a yellow kite?" Then, fearing that I might again repeat what I had said so many times before, he added, "Maybe He doesn't think I'm too young."

"Yes," I said. "We will leave it up to Him to decide about it once and for all." I was tired of the whole thing and hoped that maybe this would make Michael stop talking about it.

Michael prayed his prayer and fell asleep with a smile on his face. As I stood there looking down at the beautiful child with the blond curls, so trusting in his faith that God would answer his little prayer, I found myself questioning God. Would He really answer such a small prayer when He had chosen not to hear any of my frantic pleas or send me any help to relieve my situation? "O God," I prayed, "please help me! Show me the way out of this dark place."

The next morning as I raised the shade in the kitchen, I stared at the sight that met my eyes—a string hanging down in front of the window. Not quite able to believe the thoughts that were being put together in my mind, I found myself running out of the back door and into the yard. There it was, a yellow kite, caught on the roof, with its string hanging down.

"Oh, thank You, God, thank You!" I repeated over and over again. I was thanking Him for the yellow kite, and I was thanking Him for the joy that was flooding into my soul. He had answered the prayer of a little boy, just a little prayer, but by answering that prayer, He had also answered my prayer for help.

Suddenly I remembered Michael. I ran to his room, scooped him up in my arms and carried him into the backyard. He was still half asleep and didn't quite know what to make of his mother who was babbling about something on the roof and saying, "Wait until you see!"

He clapped his hands and bounced up and down in my arms when he saw the kite. "Mommy, Mommy, and it's even yellow!" he exclaimed. I smiled at him and added, "It's a miracle too." He hugged me and said, "I knew God would answer my prayer. I just knew He would."

I thought to myself, *This is why I have been so depressed. I lost my faith. I turned my back on God, and then insisted that He had stopped caring.*

But the yellow kite was not the only miracle that God sent to us that morning.

When Bill came home we took the kite to the beach and flew it. It went so high that it was almost out of sight for a while. Bill said he had never seen a kite fly as high. We asked all over the neighborhood but we never found a trace of the kite's former owner.

We moved several times in the years that followed, and the yellow kite always went with us. My depression left me and as my health improved, so did my relationship with my husband.

At each new place I would hang the kite in some corner where I could see it as I went about my duties. It served as a reminder that no matter how bad things may seem, we must never lose sight of the fact that God cares, that He hears our prayers. No request is too big or too small to bring before Him.

—*Beverly Newman*

God Makes A Path

God makes a path, provides a guide,
  And feeds a wilderness;
His glorious name, while breath remains,
  O that I may confess.

Lost many a time, I have had no guide,
  No house but a hollow tree!
In stormy winter night no fire,
  No food, no company;

In Him I found a house, a bed,
  A table, company;
No cup so bitter but's made sweet,
  Where God shall sweetening be.

—*Roger Williams*

Back from Yesterday

The mystery of the whereabouts of Uncle Alex stirred my imagination as a little girl and was the big topic at family reunions for nearly forty years. The mystery was resolved after World War II in a most unusual way.

Uncle Alex was my father's oldest brother. There were seven children in the Clukie family living on a farm near Standish, Michigan, many years ago. Dad loved to tell about the lazy summer days when he and Alex fished in the little stream that ran through Standish. The only problem in their lives was their mother's blindness. My grandmother was a French Canadian of great courage, however, and kept her seven children well cared for despite her handicap.

Then, one bitter cold winter my grandfather died suddenly of pneumonia. Alex, the oldest child, was only twelve at the time. With no one to manage the farm, Grandmother had to sell it. She found a job as a cook in a private home where she was allowed to keep her youngest child with her. But the other six children had to be split up with different families around the state.

Yet the Clukie children kept in touch with each other and their mother through family reunions each year—except that no one knew what had become of Alex. They were sure he had been adopted by a family named Bird, but the Birds had moved out of the state shortly afterward and no amount of tracing could discover where they had gone. Dad wrote to the postmasters of cities in nearby states, he put ads in newspapers, he talked to the police—with no success.

I remember discussions around the table at Christmas when my aunts and uncles would be together: "Alex must have died of the diphtheria that first winter and the Birds just couldn't bear to tell us" . . . "More likely he was killed in the war somewhere in France" . . . "No, I feel sure he's alive somewhere." But nobody really knew, and to my generation Uncle Alex was an almost mythical figure.

I recall the summer day in 1946 when it all came to a head. I was grown up by this time, with a family of my own. The Clukie clan was holding our annual picnic in a park by the Augres River. From all corners of the state we convened, with our baskets of cold chicken and our homemade pies.

Grandmother Clukie had died a few years earlier, but there was quite a crowd of us now: her children and grandchildren and great-grandchildren, with their husbands and wives. But as far as Dad was concerned, there was still an empty spot at the picnic table. "It just isn't fair," he said suddenly, "that Alex can't be sharing all this with us."

Dad was an especially religious man. As a child I remember Dad praying for me whenever I was sick. He had a gift for healing. Now for the first time, that afternoon, he began to talk about God's ability to heal a broken family.

Sitting there at the picnic table, he suggested a prayer contract to us: Every day for a period of one year each of us would pray that—if Alex was alive—some way, somehow, God would bring him back to us. We all agreed to take part.

Thus our year of prayer began.

And as we prayed, God—on His part—began to act. Later, looking back and comparing many notes, we were able to reconstruct the amazing sequence of events:

First, God brought a young Michigan man named Tom MacDonald to Lowry Air Force Base way out in Denver, Colorado. There in Denver, Tom met a girl whom he liked very much. Her name was Millicent Bird. When Tom and Millicent became engaged, Tom suggested that he, Millicent and her parents drive east to Michigan to meet his folks.

Millicent's father, Alex Bird, was delighted at the idea. He believed that he had never been to Michigan. The Birds were a happy, fairly typical family—except for one strange circumstance. Alex suffered from amnesia. He had absolutely no memory of anything that had happened to him before the age of twenty.

As the Birds and Tom planned their trip east, an unusual thing occurred. From Denver to Tom's home in southern Michigan is a straight drive over main highways. At an odd urging that none of them understood, they decided not to take this logical, direct route, but instead to make a long detour into Canada, come across the Straits of Mackinaw and down the whole length of Michigan. It was a roundabout way to go, but not one of them questioned it.

As they marked the road on their map, nobody noticed a little town called Standish through which their route now lay. But this is how it happened that in July 1947, a week short of one year after a certain prayer campaign began, Alex Bird came back to his childhood home.

When their car approached the town of Standish, strange sensations began pricking Alex. As the grain elevator loomed on the horizon, these feelings grew stronger. At last where the highway crossed a little fishing stream, he could keep silent no longer.

"Slow down a second, Tom," he said. "There's something about this town . . ."

Tom pulled over to the curb while Alex stared up and down the single main street. "Would you wait here just a minute?" he asked the others.

Then Alex stepped out of the car and walked slowly up the street he had not seen for forty years. Some of the houses looked vaguely familiar; others did not. In front of the old corner grocery he paused. What was there about this store?

He shook his head and continued on down the sidewalk. So

many times in Denver he had been seized by this same feeling of half-remembered places. So often he had eagerly approached some stranger, only to meet with a blank stare. So many hopes, so many disappointments. And so how could this little town in faraway Michigan have any meaning for him?

He turned and retraced his steps. But a second time in front of the little grocery he stopped short. Taking a deep breath, he walked in.

A very old man looked up from behind a crowded counter.

"I, uh—" Alex stopped, embarrassed. "I need a few packs of gum."

"There on the left," the old man said. He stared at Alex curiously. Alex's heart gave a bound. After all these years, was someone going to recognize him?

"You got a brother named Joe Clukie?" the grocer asked.

Alex's heart sank. "No. My name is Bird."

The old man shook his head. "Well, you sure are his double then," he replied. He dropped the gum into a sack. "Joe was in here recently on his way fishing up north. Lives down in Flint now."

Alex reached for his package, disappointed. But the grocer gripped the little sack, eyes far away. "I've got a picture of Joe taken the year his Pa died." He rummaged in a cluttered drawer and drew out a curling yellow photograph. It showed a man and a woman standing stiffly in their Sunday best near a staircase of dark-haired children. Alex took the picture, but it told him nothing.

"That's Joe there," the grocer said, coming around to the front of the counter. "And this little shaver is Bill. He lives in Bay City now." His finger moved to the top of the staircase. "The oldest boy's name was Alex. He used to come in here for his Ma. She couldn't see too good, the mother couldn't."

Alex was struggling with a tightness in his throat. "And where does Alex Clukie live?" he asked.

The old man shook his head. "A lot of folks would like to know that! Alex turned up missing—oh, years ago—after their Pa died."

From the only restaurant in Standish, Alex placed phone calls to William Clukie in Bay City and to my dad, Joseph Clukie, in Flint. Dad was out on his stonemason job and it took

Mother a while to find him. And so it was Bill who arrived first at the little cafe in Standish.

Bill recognized his older brother at once, but to Alex it was a stranger who seized his hand so warmly, talking about a daily prayer and a solemn agreement and a whole family waiting. Then Dad arrived and Alex had to believe, for seeing him was like looking into a mirror. Dad was shorter, but they had the same straight black hair, the smiling brown eyes, the dark complexion inherited from their Canadian mother.

Dad brought them all back to Flint to spend the night and it was there that I first met my fabled Uncle Alex. He was a man in a daze. He still did not remember the brothers and sisters who now crowded around him. He never did recall his childhood completely, nor any part of his life with the Birds.

But a remark by one of the others would bring back isolated incidents. That first evening Dad suddenly cried out:

"Alex, remember the time you backed into the stove? You've got a scar like a 'C' on the back of your right leg!"

Alex pulled up his trouser leg. There on the calf was a crescent-shaped purple mark. "So that's what it was," he said slowly. "I always wondered."

Somehow this physical, tangible link with his past seemed suddenly to make it real for Alex. The crinkles around his eyes deepened, he moved around the room clasping one hand after another in a joy too deep for words.

His wife was as thrilled as he. Again and again they urged us to visit them out in Denver. And so we did, many, many times in the years that followed. But no reunion ever topped the one we had that first summer, a year to the day after the promise was made. Again the air was sweet with pies, the baskets heavy with chicken. But this time the empty place at the table was filled. Before we started eating, Dad spoke for us all:

"For a whole year we've said a prayer, every one of us, every day. I've said it so often I didn't think I could stop. But I've got a better prayer now. Just 'Thank You, God. Thank You!' "

—Iloree Wilson

Those Fish!

If you come to our house these days, you'll find a fish mobile dangling over our kitchen table. Those fish swinging in the air always remind me of the *real* fish that insisted on entering our lives. And I never fail to remember the dreary night that I reluctantly took that first batch of fish from the freezer . . .

"This is the last straw," I muttered angrily as I slapped at the hot grease that had just spattered my arm. The pungent odor of fish frying permeated my kitchen, and I had been battling waves of nausea already.

Those fish had been in the freezer for a month, the meager results of the last fishing trip the boys had with their father. The four intervening weeks since then had been the worst of my life. Now, looking at those fish I was about to serve, I thought grimly, *I'm not that hungry.*

Well, I *was* that hungry, for with the exception of a pound of ground meat, designated for Sunday's dinner, we had nothing else to eat. Monday was payday, so we had survived the month, but no one in his right mind would term this victorious living. What about God's promises to meet our needs? Philippians 4:19, for instance? "But my God shall supply all your need according to his riches in glory by Christ Jesus." *Probably another fairy story, like living happily ever after,* I thought bitterly. I was fool enough to believe that one too.

Fred and I had such high ideals and dreams when we married, but his habit of taking a "social drink" had gradually developed into a real drinking problem, and we'd finally lost everything we owned. I'd taught school before our three sons were born, and when our youngest entered kindergarten, I returned to teaching to provide a stable income. But Fred's drinking became even more intense, culminating in full-scale alcoholism that tore our family apart. Reluctantly I filed for divorce. And one month ago my marriage of thirteen years was declared null and void.

Now my sons and I were left with the choice between these unappetizing fish—or nothing at all. Worse, it seemed indicative of a future that didn't promise anything better. So the boys came in, and eat those fish we did.

After dinner I was left alone with my worries, staring at the months ahead. Almost unconsciously my thoughts turned into a grumbled prayer: *Lord, if You don't help us, there's no way we're going to make it.*

Suddenly I was aware of an unearthly stillness that filled the kitchen. The presence of Jesus was very real, and I seemed to hear clearly the command: *Make a list of all the things you're so worried about.*

"That's easy," I replied. I grabbed a pencil and paper and wrote: House payment, new glasses for Grady, gym shoes for Woody, jeans for David, groceries . . .

Then the same Presence brought to mind the verse from Matthew: "Take no thought for your life, what ye shall eat, or what ye shall drink; nor yet for your body, what ye shall put on . . . But seek ye first the kingdom of God, and his righteousness; and all these things shall be added unto you" (6:25, 33).

I looked at the list. Every item fell neatly into one of these categories.

"Lord, that's easy to believe when things are going all right," I protested. "But I'm alone now, scratching to make ends meet. Like tonight. We had nothing left to eat."

And then I thought, *We* did *have those fish.*

A few months later soft autumn sunlight warmed our church pew where I sat, insides churning, palms sweaty. The choir was singing heartily, but I couldn't concentrate on the music or the words. I could only concentrate on that offering plate, coming closer and closer. We were broke. Although Fred was legally responsible for child support, he never contributed any money at all, which left my sons and me a monthly income of five hundred dollars. After the bills, we were left with exactly one hundred. And if I gave my tithe of fifty dollars . . . that would leave me the choice of getting shoes that two of the boys desperately needed—or buying food. I held the check in my hand as the plate got closer and closer. How could God want me to have to make this choice?

Take no thought for your life, came the whisper again.

"But my boys," I protested.

Take no thought . . .

The usher handed me the plate. I dropped in the check.

I didn't feel relieved or virtuous. In fact, when we got home,

I was a portrait of self-pity. I stopped again in the kitchen, staring at a can of tomatoes, wondering how to turn it into a meal, when there was a knock on the door. There stood my friend Betty Jean, and in her hands was a pan of fish. "Carolyn and I cooked fish together and had these left over. I can't refreeze them. Can you and the boys use them?"

Those fish. We had a wonderful meal. More than we could eat.

That year, for the first time in my life, I dreaded Christmas. Every carol, every holiday symbol brought bittersweet memories of happier times. Of course, our budget was stretched to the limit, but we'd get by. Then, without warning, I had a blowout on the old station wagon. I got the car home and put on the spare.

Dejected already, I couldn't bear to stay in the house just then, surrounded by ghosts of Christmases past. I absentmindedly got in the car and drove to the supermarket. I got a cart and walked the aisles without purpose. I thought it would help to be surrounded by piped-in carols and bustle and people, but it just made me feel more alone. So alone.

I felt a touch on my shoulder and heard a friendly voice behind me.

"Why, Peggy, it's so good to see you! How in the world are you and those boys? By the way, do they like fish? Ed just came home with another catch, and I have no more room in my freezer. I was just wondering what to do with them."

Those fish. I had to smile. I knew the spare would be okay until I could afford a new tire. I also realized that, regardless of what I felt, I was *not* alone.

For over two years we got along all right; just barely, but we got along. My frustration and self-pity abated a little at a time. And then—*whop!* I got the worst case of mumps on record. Never had I been so sick! I would see the boys off to school, then collapse on the sofa for the rest of the day. My fellow teachers took turns bringing in our supper, but my convalescence seemed to go on forever. Discouragement enveloped me again. And then my co-worker Mary put a pot of chili on the stove and came out to the den where I was resting miserably.

"Peggy," she said, "I know this sounds awful right now, but

if you'll tell me where your freezer is, I'd like to leave a catch of fish that you can cook up when you're feeling better."

Those fish!

I'm sure she thought I was delirious as I began to laugh joyfully. Now I couldn't help but remember the many times Jesus used fish to minister to the needs of people as He walked this earth. He fed the multitude of five thousand with five loaves and two fish, and again the four thousand with seven loaves and a few fish. After His resurrection, to reassure His faithful followers, He asked for some fish, and ate with them. Later, at the Sea of Galilee He cooked fish for His disciples and called Peter back into service. And He'd never forgotten *us* in our time of need.

I looked at Mary, where she still stood, amazed. "Thanks a lot for the fish," I told her. "As a matter of fact, I'm feeling better already." And do you know, I really *was* feeling better.

Fish in the freezer. This was exactly where I'd started, grumbling, those years before, so alone and bitter. Again the freezer was stocked. We'd come full circle. But how much I'd changed.

I wasn't the only one. Soon after, three years following our divorce, I received a letter from Fred. God had taken care of him, too. He told how he had spent the past fifteen months at The Anchorage, a Christian rehabilitation center for alcoholics. While there, he'd come to rely on God, and his life had been changed. He asked our forgiveness and sent us some money. From that day on, he began to help with our financial needs.

Eventually Fred and I were remarried in the little chapel at The Anchorage. I had prayed that the Lord would be faithful and save our marriage. Instead, he was faithful to save *us,* and made a new marriage with new people. The hopeless end for us was God's beginning.

Indeed, if you come to see us these days, you'll find that fish mobile over our kitchen table, a reminder that if we seek God first, everything else really will be provided. And when visitors like you notice it, as they usually do, I have a wonderful chance to tell them how God once again used fish to minister to the needs of His people.

—*Peggy Wood Stewart*

The Problem of the Barn

It was one of those gorgeous summer weekends on my parents' western New York farm. As I sat sipping coffee and looking out the kitchen window, my eyes went from porch to tree, bush to garden, as I remembered little childhood hiding places and play areas. Myriad emotions tugged me in different directions as I stared out at those childhood hideaways. For one thing, I was making mental plans for my upcoming wedding—delightful plans for colors and flowers and duplicate toasters. But then my eyes rested on the barn and I felt that sick feeling again. Was I *really* going to walk out of my parents' lives at a time like this?

"What are you sitting here worrying about?" Mom had come up behind me, and gave her worrier a warm hug. She always knew thinking from worrying, somehow.

"Oh . . . that barn," I said.

"I knew it," she shook her head in sympathy. "Well, let's not trouble ourselves on this beautiful day. The Lord will help us think of something. Why don't you have a piece of this cake? I want you to take some back to your apartment, too."

Wasn't that just like Mom! Leave everything to the Lord, set aside things that need to be struggled with, and make sure everyone has cake.

That barn! It stood a dizzying three stories high. It had been designed well over a hundred years ago to accommodate livestock and hay and for fruit storage. But since my parents were no longer working the farm, they used it only to store machinery and tools. And the many winters and springs—the howling, rainy winds and snowstorms—had taken their toll on the barn despite Dad's attempts to patch and repair. Seeping water had caused the old stone-and-concrete foundation to begin moving and crumbling away from the wooden walls, leaving gaps. Frayed wiring provided electricity to the barn, the yellowed bulbs shining upon old stored papers and junk. And the firetrap stood uncomfortably close to the house.

Yet how difficult to think of the barn as a hazard, when I
could remember so well the smell of the sun-warm boards of
this, my haunted castle, my dance studio, my Kentucky stables.
I had watched Dad build things in that barn, with his treasury
of shining tools and evil-sounding machines. I had drawn with
chalk on the great sliding doors, painted my bike red on the
west step. In the loft I'd even composed a love song that now
caused me to blush. But the usefulness of my barn-friend for
play or for work had ended. It perched on its precarious
points, waiting.

Dad came into the kitchen, blinking and sniffing deeply. He
knew that the time had come for the barn to go. As I sat down
across from him, I felt an aching sadness. So much was changing—even Dad. Something in me tried to force into my mind
the image of Dad as he used to be: muscular, jet-black hair,
large-featured handsomeness; the rider of motorcycles,
builder of things, inventor. There was so much for me to be
wildly proud of as a child—and I was still proud of him. But
the graying man before me seemed smaller, older somehow.

"Dad," I began carefully, "what do you suppose it would
cost to hire someone to take that barn down for you?"

"More'n I've got," he quipped. (I already knew the direction this conversation was going.)

"How about if we got some men from the church to help
us do it?"

"I don't want anyone getting hurt on that thing."

"What about you?" I demanded. "I don't want you to get
hurt either!"

"I haven't broken my neck on The Ark yet." Dad chuckled
and settled back into his chair as if to close the subject. He had
taken to calling the aging barn "The Ark." And a more stubborn Noah, I mused, there never was.

"Dad, I could help with the money. We could hire someone—"

"No!" He sat bolt upright now. "I got a certain way I want
it done. The top beams can't be sawed or broken. I'm going
to use them on the new garage I'm going to build. I know how
wrecking crews like to do things. No, by ginger!"

"But Dad . . ."

"Me and the Lord can take down The Ark." I knew by the

way he sat back and looked away that the subject was very much closed.

"I'm going to come home every weekend and help 'you and the Lord,' Dad," I informed him. I didn't know how, though. One of us was a thin office girl with a built-in fear of heights.

That next Saturday I arrived early, and Dad met me at the porch door. He had to smile at my work clothes and determined expression.

"I figure we'll start taking things out today," he said. We spent the weekend sifting through dusty objects. There were books, bottomless chairs, chicken feeders, rusty veterinary objects. We walked about carefully in the waspy attic, feeling the slight sway of the structure. We laughed at old feedbag designs, argued over what was or wasn't an antique, told stories connected with some of the curios we found, such as the cougar-shaped lamp (which an uncle had won at the carnival).

After two weekends of sifting and sorting, we had the shed full of salvageable things and a great heap to be burned. The two tractors and their attachments had been placed in an easily accessible area just inside the barn's basement door. Much equipment still remained inside; we had barely scratched the surface, even though most of the valuable things had been removed. But we still faced the main goal of getting the old barn torn down.

That Sunday evening I again stood staring at the looming structure. Mom and Dad were an acre away, walking arm in arm, checking on their fruit trees. They had begun to call this "taking the tour." I could hear them arguing coyly and good-naturedly about how the apple trees should be trimmed, a topic on which they never agreed. They seemed totally oblivious to the problem of the barn. Watching their distant forms move on to the next group of trees—these parents whom I loved so fiercely—I felt as if I were the mother hen and they the wandering, curious chicks, wobbling into misfortune before I could see and intervene. Often, lately, I was annoyed with them for neglecting themselves; for not eating better; for growing older.

I sat on the grass now, feeling helpless. I would be getting married in less than two months. Soon after the honeymoon, I would be leaving for the West, where my husband would finish college. How would this leveling of the barn ever get done? Shouldn't I be there where I was really needed? And yet what good would my frail presence be on a job such as this? It all seemed so hopeless.

In the weeks that followed, I got caught up in the colorful commotion of preparing for a wedding. When I wasn't busy with lists and errands, I would pause and think happily of the wonderful tall blond landscape architect who was making it all possible: Michael. Together we reveled in the great heap of bridal shower gifts (he complained to me that fishing equipment was never a present—just kitchen stuff). We made plans, phone calls and occasionally retreated to the movies.

I put the barn problem aside for the most part, remembering it occasionally and then following Mom around whining about what could happen. She would shake her head, admitting that she had no answers for me. She simply said, "Let's leave it with the Lord."

The wedding day came and went in a joyous, kaleidoscopic blur. We were off, then, on a carefree month-long honeymoon, camping like gleeful gypsies around the perimeter of Nova Scotia. Swept away with the patchwork landscape of eastern Canada and my brand-new husband, tan and tousled from walking the warm beaches, I admit I gave not one fleeting thought to the barn.

Soon it was time to begin the drive back home. I could hardly wait to tell the folks of clam-digging, and the day we made chowder in a bucket; of ferry rides and people we'd met—like John and Alex, the coal miners who came and sat and sang for us at our campfire.

Finally we reached the town of Ripley. One by one we passed the friendly old landmarks: the stately school, Rice's Hardware Store, State Street's tracks.

As we rounded the curve of our tree-lined driveway, my eyes saw the sight, but my brain reeled with disbelief. There, where the huge barn had towered, was a flat, squatty pile of rubble with the roof on top of it all. Dad was grinning from atop that roof when we drove in, and he hopped to the ground with welcoming shouts.

Mom hurried out, a damp dish towel in her hands, and soon we were hugging and kissing and in the midst of it all I couldn't help but marvel at how Dad had managed to get the barn down.

"Had a big windstorm last week," he said. "The Lord decided to take 'er down without my help. And lookit . . . there . . ."

I gazed in wonder as he pointed to the peaked portion of the roof that had gently protected the tractors when the structure collapsed. "Not only is the equipment okay, but look at these roof beams."

I walked over to see that not one beam had been broken in the fall. Dad could disassemble them while standing barely four feet off the ground. And yet the happy expressions on my parents' faces were not ones of awe, just faithful satisfaction. And that was how they smiled at me now, as I stood with Michael's arm gently around my shoulder.

"Funniest thing is," Dad chuckled, lowering his head and scrunching up his shoulders like a mischievous little boy, "she never made much of a sound when she went! We slept right through the whole dang thing!"

And little wonder. If the Lord took this good care of my trusting parents, He surely wouldn't wish to disturb their sleep.

—Kathie Kania

The Deer in the City

I'd once been an active man, a man who knew how to walk in the woods. Even in the dark I could find my way to the wild brook, where I'd be fishing by dawn, able to see deer come down from the mountain to drink.

By 1980 those woodland days were over. For more than fifteen years I'd been confined to a wheelchair, a victim of crippling rheumatoid arthritis. I did my best to live a full life, and I still felt loved by God. Just the same, when November's sporting season came round, I tended to be bitter.

One November Saturday a few old hunting buddies came over. The season wasn't due to open for a few days, but they were on their way to Clark's Valley just to scout for deer. They were all excited. They said they would see a deer for me.

"Thanks," I said, "but I'd really like to see one myself." My buddies couldn't reply to that.

That afternoon I sat in my wheelchair and tried to watch a football game on TV, but I kept thinking of tramping in Clark's Valley. The game ended and I didn't even know who'd won. I closed my eyes and threw myself a pity party, wanting so badly to be out there where I could see a deer.

At last I reopened my eyes and looked out our picture window. There, on my lawn, staring straight into my eyes, stood the biggest buck I'd ever seen. I called to my wife. Ginny came running. She saw too.

The buck stared at me a moment longer, then loped silently away, his big rack spread wide like angel wings. Right here in Harrisburg, Pennsylvania's capital city.

—*Norman Strawser*

Bees to the Rescue

I came into the office of our Connecticut farm hoping that my feelings weren't showing on my face. Evidently they weren't, because my wife, Lois, who was signing payroll checks, murmured "Hello, dear," and went right on working. I sat down in my old swivel chair, swung it around, locked my hands behind my head and stared out across the road at the buildings that housed some of our farm equipment. *Retirement.* The word tolled like a funeral bell in my mind.

I had come from a meeting with my sons, who helped me run our four-hundred–acre farm. We had discussed my most recent visit to the heart specialist. The boys already knew about the angina attack I'd had a few months before. And they had told me, kindly but firmly, that in view of my age and heart condition, they thought—and the doctor agreed—that I should let them take charge of the farm.

Retirement. Maybe some folks who dislike their work look forward to it. But the farm had been my life for more than seventy years. Being told to give it up was like a sentence of death . . . slow death.

Where had they gone, all those good years? How could they have flown by so fast? I had been born in the old farmhouse, which was just a few yards from where I was sitting now. As a little boy, in my first pair of overalls, I had followed my dad around the farm till I was old enough to take on some of the chores myself. I could remember it all so clearly: hoeing the crops of tobacco under the hot summer sun; digging potatoes and putting them into the heavy wooden barrels; feeding the chickens and grading the eggs during the evening hours after the other chores. All these tasks brought strength to my growing body and steadiness to my mind.

The farm became part of me as I became part of the farm. I learned to love the smell of newly turned earth and the freshness of crops sprinkled with morning dew. I felt the nearness and the power of God as I planted the tiny seeds that He would cause to grow into the food we ate. I saw His plan for the earth in the changing seasons, in the parched fields just before He sent the badly needed rain. I learned to pray through the destruction of crops, which sometimes came with the summer hails and high winds of our New England storms.

When my dad became too ill to work, I took over the farm, increasing its size, raising shade-grown tobacco, Katahdin potatoes, and several varieties of trees and nursery plants. Our operation expanded until we were employing almost three hundred youths and adults during the peak summer season. It became a thriving business that supported not only our immediate family, but the families of our nephew and several other dependable workers as well.

Perhaps having total responsibility for so large an enterprise *was* too demanding for someone my age, but it brought me nothing but contentment. Every morning at six I would leave our house just down the road and come to this office to discuss the day's work with my sons and helpers. Then throughout the day I'd make the rounds of fields and sheds, keeping an eye on things. An experienced and watchful eye, I hoped. How could I give this up? A spark of something like anger flashed through me. Suppose I just refused to change my way of life? After all, no one could force me. But would that be selfish?

Would it be unfair to the younger family members? Or to Lois? "O Lord," I found myself praying, "please show me what to do."

Behind me Lois's voice spoke softly. "You're awfully quiet, Emil. Is anything wrong?"

I've never been able to keep anything from Lois, so I told her. She didn't say much. She came over and rested her hands on my shoulders. I knew she was distressed for me, but I also knew that a part of her—the loving, protective part—thought that maybe my sons and my doctor were right.

Outside the office, as we talked, one of the green farm buses pulled into the parking area. Through the window we watched as some of the young Puerto Rican men we had hired spilled out, laughing, chattering, still full of energy and good humor after their day of trimming evergreens. They were good workers; we had grown fond of them. Now half a dozen came crowding through the office door, dark eyes sparkling with excitement. "Mr. Emil! Mr. Emil! *Venga a ver! Una cosa Maravillosa!*"

Gradually, in a mixture of Spanish and broken English, they were able to make me understand what they had found: a swarm of bees in a tree near the place they had been working. They wanted to know if I knew how to capture them—and, as a matter of fact, I did.

When I was a boy of twelve, a neighbor had helped me build a wooden box for a swarm of bees I had found in an old dump. After that I had had good luck with raising bees and knew quite a lot about them.

So I asked my son Len to go with me and together we borrowed an empty hive from a friend not far away who was a beekeeper. We cut the bran h that held the swarm and placed it in front of the hive. The odor from the comb inside the hive attracted the queen bee, and the rest of the swarm followed her inside. While Lois watched from a safe distance, we settled the hive and its humming occupants in a sheltered spot behind some hemlocks near our house.

When Len had gone back to work, I stood there looking at our new acquisition. Something seemed to be tugging at a corner of my memory, and all of a sudden a scene from my childhood rose up out of the past. I was sixteen years old, and by now I had acquired twenty-four hives of bees. I cared for them myself, extracting the honey, bottling it and selling it in nearby towns or agricultural fairs, a three-pound jar for a dollar. On this day, when I was busy extracting honey, my mother came into the shed where I was working, and she was crying. Alarmed, I asked her if she was in some kind of pain.

"No," she said, "I feel all right. But Emil, there's something you don't know about. Two days from now, the payment on our farm mortgage is due. I need fifty-five dollars to pay it, and all we have in the world is thirty-six dollars and seventy cents. I've tried and tried to save, but I just can't scrape up any more." Suddenly she covered her face with her hands. "O Lord," she said in a choking voice, "please show us what to do. Please help us."

The moment she said that, the thought came to me that the answer to the problem might be right here, in the honey from my bees. "Mom!" I said. "Don't cry. Tomorrow I'll take this honey over to Rockville and see if I can bring back the money you need."

I worked late that night, extracting and bottling the honey. The next day, after my trip to Rockville, I brought back not only the amount needed to meet the payment, but an extra seven dollars that I gave my mother to use for other expenses. And she cried again, this time for joy.

Standing there by the hive, I was amazed at how vivid this recollection was. Almost half a century ago, my mother had asked the Lord to show her what to do—and through the bees had come the answer. This very day, in my own despair, I had prayed the identical prayer, and again the response seemed to take the form of a swarm of bees.

Coincidence? I don't think so. I think the Lord was telling me that the time had come for a switch from a complex and demanding job to a more tranquil and placid form of activity, such as beekeeping. I think He was giving me a new direction to follow.

Today I'm happy keeping bees and leaving the management of the farm—well, *almost* all of it—to the boys. What I've learned is this: If you have a need or a problem and ask the

Lord to show you what to do, He will show you. One way or another. Even with something as unexpected as a swarm of bees.

—Emil Molnite
as told to *Lois Molnite*

Our Refuge

Whenever you come to the Lord
  with an earnest prayer,
He is there.
When you come with a contrite heart
  or a human fear,
He will hear.
Though you may have little to give,
  bring Him your best;
He supplies the rest.

—Nina Willis Walter

GOD PROTECTS

God is our refuge and strength, a very present help in trouble.
—Psalm 46:1

When we look at all the stories in *His Mysterious Ways*, we see that God doesn't work in just one way. Sometimes He lets us get into trouble and rescues us from it. But sometimes He keeps us out of danger, or prevents some major disaster from happening.

God protects us in many ways. There are times when He sends us messages and clues—like hunches, or strange sounds. Often the clues need interpreting. Always they need our response in action. Sometimes He uses the prayers of others. Sometimes he uses His "angels," who appear again in this section, coming mysteriously out of nowhere to separate us from trouble and danger.

These stories remind us that God's protection is around us all the time—at home, at work, in our travels: "It is of the Lord's mercies that we are not consumed . . ." (Lamentations 3:22). We travel safely every day on busy streets and highways, in cars and buses and subway trains and on foot. We safely use electricity and gas for cooking and to heat and light our homes. Yet, uncontrolled, these substances can destroy us and our homes. God's protection surrounds us even when we are unconscious of it: "Great is thy faithfulness" (Lamentations 3:23).

"Someone's in Trouble!"

It was a hot summer morning. *Hermano* Pablo* and four other Christian ministers climbed into Pablo's ancient Chevrolet to travel through the foothills of El Salvador. For several days they'd been conducting revival meetings out in the country; now they were headed for San Salvador, the capital city.

The trip over the narrow, twisting roads was hazardous even under good weather conditions. But conditions that morning were far from good. Summer is the rainy season in El Salvador, and in many places the dirt road had already turned to mud. Worse, none of the five men in the car knew this region. They did not know that about a hundred fifty miles ahead of them, around a deceptive curve, lay the tracks of a railroad.

That same morning, many miles away in the city of Santa Ana, an Indian housemaid was having trouble settling down to work. Angela Mancia kept stopping in the middle of her chores.

Angela worked for a missionary couple, Ralph and Jewel Williams. She knew *Hermano* Pablo well—he always stayed with the Williamses when he was in Santa Ana—and Angela often prayed for him and his work. But she was not thinking about him that morning. Indeed, she was aware only of a vague uneasiness, a mounting sense of fear.

Hermano Pablo was driving with one eye on the thunderclouds massing in the east. His friends—Israel Garcia beside him in the front seat, Juan, Jose and Fernando in back—watched the approaching storm as they talked.

About eleven o'clock the rain reached them, the tropical storm lashing the windshield faster than the wipers could sweep it clean. Pablo leaned forward, straining to see ahead.

Angela was struggling with unaccountable tears when Jewel Williams walked into the kitchen. "Angela! What on earth's the matter?"

*Missionary Paul Finkenbinder.

159

"I don't know, señora," Angela insisted. "Except—" and all at once she was sure of something. "Someone's in trouble! I know it! Do you think . . . do you think I should go to the church and pray?"

Of course! So Angela started up the muddy street to the little church where she and the Williams family worshiped.

Ordinarily it took about ten minutes to climb the hill. But that morning it took Angela half an hour because she stopped to talk to every Christian friend she met. To each she described the strange uneasiness, the growing sureness that God was telling her to pray for someone.

"Won't you come with me?" she asked each one. Half a dozen women agreed. And so it was that morning that a handful of Indian Christians walked through the door of the little Assembly of God church, sat down and began to pray without knowing what it was they were praying about.

At about one o'clock the five ministers stopped for lunch. The rain continued. Outside, the road was growing more slippery every minute. They climbed back into the old car and went on.

In Santa Ana, the pendulum clock on the wall of the church read 1:30. The women prayed without stopping to eat, unaware of hunger, unaware of anything except the urgency that now gripped them all. "Lord, somewhere one of Your children is in trouble. You know who it is, Lord Jesus. Put Your hand where the need is."

It was like driving inside a drum, Pablo thought—with the rain hammering on the roof. It was nearly dark as a drum, too, although it was only two in the afternoon. Pablo decided to stop until the storm was over. But where? Up ahead he made out a curve. Just beyond it, perhaps, there'd be a place to pull over.

"Help Your child, Lord, wherever he is!"

"Look out!" Israel Garcia cried.
The headlight of a train loomed from nowhere out of the

storm, coming fast. Pablo jerked the wheel and slammed on the brakes, but the car kept sliding over the slick mud.

They heard the frantic scream of the whistle. Then the locomotive hit them. The car spun around, and the train hit it again. The right-hand door flew open; Garcia was hurled out. The car rose into the air, came down on its top and turned over.

"Help him, Lord!"

Pablo opened his eyes. He was lying on the ground, and the rain had stopped. Beside him was a tangle of metal that only gradually he recognized as his Chevy.

Now he realized that he was delirious. Because it seemed to him that a crowd of people was standing around him, and that among them were his four friends—all alive and all talking to a policeman, who was making notes in a little book. The engineer of the train was there, too, staring at them.

"The time!" the policeman was asking him.

The engineer drew a watch from his pocket, still staring at the four. In the voice of one dazed, he replied, "It's two-thirty."

Slowly, shakily, Pablo got to his feet. "It's not possible," the engineer began. Pablo was embracing his friends. At the policeman's orders they started for the ambulance, walking away from the circle of gaping passengers, away from the still throbbing locomotive, away from the sound of the engineer's voice saying, "How can it be! No one could have walked out of that car! It isn't possible!"

Far away in Santa Ana, the long prayer vigil was over.

A sudden silence fell over the church. Angela opened her eyes and looked around. The haunted feeling was gone.

The other women felt it too. They knew that whatever they had been called to do was now finished.

Angela's voice was a little tired as she spoke. Almost in a whisper she suggested that they sing a hymn of praise and thanksgiving. "I'd like to sing, 'How Great Thou Art,' " she said—and then for the first time she remembered the work waiting for her back at the house.

Angela glanced at the pendulum clock and was astonished to see how late it was. The clock's hands stood at 2:30.

—John and Elizabeth Sherrill

To One Who Prayed

Dear friend:
Last night I know you touched
With prayer's firm fingertips
My tensely furrowed brow
And tight-drawn lips.
For that dark grief that clutched
My heart in its cold steel fist
Had gone when I awoke,
With not a twist.

A stronger hand of love
Had loosed that grip and healed
The hurt—such power can faith
Reach out and wield!
An awesome Presence filled
My soul with life anew.
Someone had cared and prayed.
Thank God—and you.

—Ellen Ross

"Am I Dreaming?"

With our four little children and two visiting nieces to tuck in, bedtime that night took a long time. Over each drowsy child I said a prayer, asking God to watch over them. Later, when my husband and I went to bed, I lay on the edge of sleep, lulled by the innocent noises drifting down the hallway: deep-sleep sighs, the mumbled words of dreamy conversations.

At 4:30 I woke up abruptly. I heard a niece whimper. Suddenly I found myself out of bed, running down the hallway. But not to the room where my niece lay. Without knowing why, I ran to my children's bedroom on the other side of the house.

I stood in their doorway, hearing my heart pounding in my ears. Something bad was about to happen. Seconds ticked by. The children went on sleeping peacefully in their bunk beds. All was so quiet. *Why did I run here? Am I dreaming?*

And then before my eyes the upper half of the bunk bed came apart. I rushed forward to catch the heavy mattress board and mattress before they crashed down onto my littlest one, Rachel, in the bottom bunk. I cried for help and my husband came; in a few moments all was set to right.

Andy and I stepped back. "Why were you in here?" he asked.

"I don't know."

"Thank God you were," Andy said. And then, with a smile, he added, "Listen, we're whispering. The kids never even woke up."

—Lynn B. Link

When Time Stood Still

When it comes to God's guidance, which it does every day, every hour, there are many ways we can seek it.

More and more often, more and more surely, with more and more conviction as my need and my faith grow, I have learned to depend on it.

Stand ye still.

Always those words come to me when I ask for guidance, wherever I happen to be, no matter how rushing and noisy it may be inside my mind and out. For to those words I owe the life of my oldest son, Mac.

One December night I awoke suddenly and completely, sitting straight up in bed. I was *sure* somebody had called me.

When I switched on the light, my clock said 3:15. Getting up, I prowled—a niece, a nephew, one younger son were sleeping in the house. Everyone seemed safe and peaceful.

I do not hear voices, nor see lights, nor catch the echo of bells. But when guidance comes, something irresistible seems to take over. Now the call was distinct in my mind—a call for help.

In the living room, I saw the Christmas tree. Next to the fireplace it stood, slim and green. Tomorrow we'd hang it with bright colors and put the Christmas angel on the top—the one that had been my grandmother's. It was the season of peace on earth, good will to men, but there was no peace on earth, this December of 1944. It was the month of the Battle of the Bulge, Bastogne, the Ardennes. My brothers were Marines in the Pacific, my oldest son in France with Patton.

I went back to bed. The call was not from within my home's safe walls. The clock now said 3:25. But it was a different time on islands in the Pacific, on the battlefields of Europe. So I did what, whenever it is possible, is my first step in asking for guidance. I got my Bible from under the detective story with which I'd read myself to sleep, shut my eyes and said, "Father, let me find Your word meant for me. I think one of Your other children needs Your help. I am far away from whoever it is, but You are near us both. Speak to us now through Your word."

In guidance, my experimentation leads me to believe that inner quietness is the first requirement. And the most difficult. Nobody wants to be quiet. Not many of us want to be silent and listen. Prayer is an audience, not an audition; nevertheless, we start telling our Father about the problem and how He ought to solve it.

That's why, when I ask for guidance, to keep my own mind still, I read something: a prayer, a book of inspiration, mostly the Bible. Then I try to be quiet for as long as I am able, in my mind I mean, which is about one minute and forty-two seconds—two minutes at the most, as it is with most people. Then I *ask,* with all the expectation and humility that I can generate.

That night I opened the Bible. Just anywhere, where it fell apart.

"Stand ye still, and see the salvation of the Lord with you
. . . fear not, nor be dismayed . . . for the Lord will be with
you" (2 Chronicles 20:17).

Stand ye still. It stood out from the page like copy on a
billboard.

And so, simply and directly, I began to pray.

I knew now from whom the call had come, as it had come
for many years in many dark nights.

"Father," I prayed, "Your guidance now goes to my son,
somewhere in battle, somewhere in danger. Your word goes
forth to him and will accomplish what You please for him,
which is his safety and his guidance, the light to his feet."

Stand ye still.

I knew, I really did, that this was my guidance and would
be my son's. That it had come to me through a channel kept
open by prayer and longing and seeking. I went back to sleep
in peace.

At breakfast, I told everyone what had taken place. Then it
came to me that as it was so near Christmas and everybody
always remembers things around Christmas, perhaps Mac
would remember something about that early morning hour.
So to his APO number I wrote, describing the experience.

His reply reached me soon after Christmas. It said, "Yes,
I can remember. I was the leader on an I&R [Intelligence
and Reconnaisance] platoon; we were out ahead of our regi-
ment, somewhere in the German area, to see if it was safe to
move forward. We were moving cautiously, but General Patton was always in a hurry so we were trotting along as fast as
we dared.

"All of a sudden it was as though something told me to stop.
To stand still. And as I did, out of the corner of my eye, I saw
a place on a tree where somebody had chopped off the bark
and scrawled in paint the word *Minen.* So I knew it was a mine
field. A German soldier had put that sign up to warn his own
troops.

"We went back faster than we'd come out, and called up the
mine detector squad and, sure enough, there were mines
enough to blow up the whole platoon, maybe the Third Army.
If I hadn't stopped (and I had to be standing dead-still to see
it because it faced the other way), I wouldn't be writing this

letter. And we wouldn't have had any Christmas, merry or otherwise."

Maybe you will have another explanation for this!

But to this day it has made a working Christian out of Mac. To me it was God's guidance. The voice of His love for us coming through to us.

The first time you receive guidance you will know the difference. You can mistake rhinestones for diamonds, but you can never mistake a diamond for a rhinestone. I know what is true guidance when my mind, my consciousness, whatever we call our mental process, is *thinking* utterly and completely with some thought that I know I have not thought. This comes when the Mind that was in Christ Jesus for which we have prayed takes over.

—*Adela Rogers St. Johns*

Reassurance

Dear Lord:

Could You spare some Guardian Angels
To give me peace of mind
As my children wander from me
And stretch the ties that bind?

You have heavenly legions, Father.
Could you send me just a few
To guide my eager youngsters
As I give them, Lord, to You?

Oh thank You, thank You, Father,
And, oh, my glad heart sings.
I'm certain that just now I heard
The swish of passing wings!

—*Betty Banner*

The Fourth Man

It had been reckless of me, taking a before-dawn stroll through the tangle of streets behind the Los Angeles bus terminal. But I was a young woman arriving in the great city for the first time. My job interview was five hours away, and I couldn't wait to explore!

Now I'd lost my way in a Skid Row neighborhood. Hearing a car pass, I turned and, in the flash of light, saw three men lurking behind me, trying to keep out of sight in the shadows. Trembling with fright, I did what I always do when in need of help. I bowed my head and asked God to rescue me.

But when I looked up, a fourth man was striding toward me in the dark! *Dear God, I'm surrounded.* I was so scared, it took me a few seconds to realize that even in the blackness I could *see* this man. He was dressed in an immaculate workshirt and denim pants, and carried a lunchbox. He was about thirty, well over six feet. His face was stern but beautiful (the only word for it).

I ran up to him. "I'm lost and some men are following me," I said in desperation. "I took a walk from the bus depot—I'm so scared."

"Come," he said. "I'll take you to safety."

He was strong and made me feel safe.

"I . . . I don't know what would have happened if you hadn't come along."

"I do." His voice was resonant, deep.

"I prayed for help just before you came."

A smile touched his mouth and eyes. We were nearing the depot. "You are safe now."

"Thank you—so much," I said fervently.

He nodded. "Good-bye, Euphie."

Going into the lobby, it hit me. *Euphie!* Had he really used my first name? I whirled, burst out onto the sidewalk. But he had vanished.

—*Euphie Eallonardo*

The Dog Who Was There

One day a dog appeared at our Iowa farm. Somehow we understood that he had come to stay. We fed him table scraps, but he did not beg for food as some dogs do, nor did he wag his tail with happiness when fed.

He did not have a distinctive coloring. His hair was brown mixed with black, his tail stubby. We did not even give him a name, perhaps because he never had to be called. He was always there. This dog seemed to think his mission in life was to accompany me as I went about the outdoor duties of a farmwife. When I fed the chickens or gathered vegetables, he was by my side. Sometimes, not only did he escort me, but he also carried one of my hands gently in his mouth.

One day a stranger came. Oddly, he parked his car midway between the house and barn. When I stepped out on the porch, he asked a question about the previous owner of our farm. Then he appeared not to hear my answer. He walked toward me and asked the question again. This time I walked out in the yard a short way before I answered him. Again he seemed not to understand and continued to walk toward me. Now I sensed that he could hear me perfectly well.

Suddenly the man came to an abrupt stop. "Will that dog bite?" he asked.

I had not realized the dog was beside me, so quietly had he come. This time he did not take my hand in his mouth. His upper lip was pulled back revealing sharp teeth.

"He certainly will," I answered firmly.

The man understood my words perfectly. He hurried to his car and drove away.

Soon after, the dog left. He may have gone to hunt rabbits and just never came back.

Somehow I do not think so.

—*Hazel Houston*

The Mangy Angel

Cold March showers pelted my face as I stepped from the warmth of the church and threaded my way across the lot toward the parsonage.

Thursday evening's meeting of the women's missionary society had finally closed, and as the pastor's wife, I was the last to leave.

My husband had gone to a general conference in Detroit, and the children and I were alone. I half expected to find the parsonage cloaked with night, for the hour was late and the children should have been in bed hours ago.

Letting myself in quietly, I was surprised to find the kitchen light still burning. Ted, our oldest, his dark head bent over his books, was studying at the table. He looked up as I came in.

"H'lo, Mom. Wet out, isn't it?"

"It's a wild night, all right," I said wryly, peeling off my dripping coat and boots.

He went back to his homework.

As I turned to leave the kitchen I looked down. Then I gasped. Our huge mangy dog lay stretched out at Ted's side!

"Ted! What's Brownie doing in the house?" I demanded. "You know he's never stayed inside before!"

Ted glanced up from his book and shrugged. "Why, he just wanted in so I let him in. Then I decided I might as well bring my homework down here."

Brownie wanted in! That, in itself, was utterly incongruous. For that matter, so was everything else about that dog.

Black, brown and smelly—and of undetermined breed—he had wandered into the parsonage one day and simply decided to stay. He adopted our family and was fiercely protective of us in every way. In fact, he loved us so much, that he wanted to be where we were. Yet, once we'd let him into the house, he developed a peculiar claustrophobic streak. He would race in terror from window to door to window until we'd let him out. No amount of bribing or petting could persuade Brownie to remain indoors. Even the dreary *drip-drip* of rain from the eaves failed to lure him inside. He preferred the most inclement outdoor weather to being enclosed.

Until now.

There he was, lying calmly beside Ted in the kitchen like a very ordinary house dog.

I remembered his previous fierce possessiveness of us. Our large, red-brick parsonage sprawled comfortably on a big grassy plot behind the church and opposite the public school. Children often cut across the church property and through our yard when hurrying to and from school. We didn't mind. In fact, they were our friends. Against our better judgment, we often had report cards thrust at us even before parents saw them.

That is, until the dog came. He growled threateningly at anyone who dared cross our yard. Yet Brownie always came when I called him off.

Still, with people dropping in at our parsonage at all hours of the day, I was afraid some day I wouldn't get him called off in time.

I tried desperately to find another home for him, but with no success. Once I even called the Humane Society.

"Sure, lady," they said. "We'll get him. But you gotta catch him and shut him up for us."

Shut Brownie up? Impossible! One might as well try to imprison a victim of claustrophobia in an elevator! Until a better solution presented itself, he would have to remain with us.

And that's how things stood that wild, stormy night I came home from church.

Shaking my head at Brownie's strange behavior, I went down to the basement to bolt the door that leads to the outside. I came back up directly and retired to the living room with the paper.

Ted already had gone up to bed, and I decided to turn in, too. The dog still lay on the kitchen floor, his shaggy head resting on his front paws.

Better put Brownie out first, I thought as I entered the kitchen to lock the back door. Rain still drummed steadily against the windows.

But when I tried to get the dog out of the door, he refused to budge. I wheedled. I coaxed. I pushed and pulled. He remained stationary.

Going to the refrigerator, I took out a chunk of meat and

tried to bribe him to the door by dangling it in front of him. He still refused to move.

With a bewildered sigh I picked up his hind end, yanked him toward the door, and out of it. Like quicksilver, his front end slid back in!

I grabbed his front end, and the back was in. His four feet seemed like a baker's dozen. Stubborn, determined, yet somehow placid. Talk about Balaam's donkey—I knew exactly how Balaam felt!

Should I call Ted to help me? No, the hour was late and Ted needed his sleep. I decided to shut all the doors to the kitchen and leave the dog inside. Then I went wearily to bed.

The next morning the dog reverted to his true nature and frantically tore out of the house.

A puzzled frown ribbed my forehead as I went down to the basement to turn on the furnace. What had made Brownie behave so strangely? Why had he been determined to remain in the house this one particular night? I shook my head. There seemed to be no answer.

When I reached the bottom of the stairs, I felt a breath of cold, damp air. Then a queer, slimy feeling swept over me. The outside door was open! Was someone in the basement?

After the first wave of panic had drained from me, my reasoning returned.

Someone had gone out of the basement!

Limp with the reality of that fact, I looked around. The windows were as snug and tight on the inside as ever. Whoever had gone out of that door had been in when I had gone down to bolt it the night before! He apparently had heard my unsuccessful attempts to put the dog out and knew he had to come up through the kitchen and face the dog—or go out the door he had come in earlier.

That smelly, stray pooch had known this, and God had used him to keep us safe. Why didn't he growl or bark? I don't know. Maybe he knew he didn't have to.

I had always believed that God has definite work for His holy angels, and that as His child I could lay claim to the verse in Hebrews 1:14: "Are they [angels] not all ministering spirits, sent forth to minister for them who shall be heirs of salvation?"

But His "ministering spirit" had taken a peculiar form that wild, stormy night. Instead of glorious, dazzling wings, the Lord had given our guardian angel four stubborn, mangy feet!

—*Esther L. Vogt*

The Cross in the Rock

The rock was bigger than a watermelon, and when I uncovered it in the field I was plowing that November, it was smudged with black earth. In the spring, I came back with a power scoop to take it away, and the winter rains and snows had washed it clean. I stared. Right on the face of that big, dark boulder, a pink cross stood out, clear as if it had been chiseled.

"Why, that's the cross of Christ," I said to myself. "This isn't going to any rock pile. It's a holy thing!"

I hauled it up to the house to show my wife, Bun, and she felt the same way I did. We got to thinking about God's telling the Israelites to keep a sign of their faith written on the doorposts of their houses (Deuteronomy 11:18–20), and we decided to set it up by our door.

Everybody who saw it thought the rock was unusual—even before we had the tornado in August 1979. Bun and I could hear the storm banging in the distance while we watched the news on TV. "Well, folks," the weatherman said, "there's a tornado watch, and my best advice is to keep an eye on the sky."

"I'll just go out and take a look," I told Bun.

And, by golly, that thing was coming right at us—a wide, black funnel cutting through my cornfield, chewing up everything in its path, moving from southwest to northeast the way tornadoes generally do.

Bun and I hid in the cellar and then the twister was on us, shaking the doors like demons from hell, the noise like an ungodly scream. We prayed. Our neighbors saw what happened.

Not once but twice that tornado came right up to our door

where the rock with the cross of Christ sat—and each time it backed away!

—*Robert M. Barr*

The Smoke Alarm

I'm sixteen years old, and ever since I was a young girl my parents told me that God is always watching over us. I believed this, but I couldn't really say that my experience had proven this to be so. *Maybe it will when I get older,* I thought.

One winter night an unexpected sound woke our household at 3:00 A.M. My father dashed down the hall, sniffing the air. My sister and I scurried to our bedroom door.

When Dad came back upstairs he said, "I don't understand it." He breathed a sigh of confusion, then returned to his room.

I couldn't go back to sleep. I went to my parent's room and said to my father, who couldn't sleep either, "Are you sure? Did you check—?"

"Yes, Tracey, I checked everything," said Dad. I started back to my room, but as I reached the door my mother suddenly cried out, "The coffee pot! I think I left the coffee pot on at church."

Earlier that evening my mother had served coffee at a church gathering. Now, in an instant, Dad was gone. Mom and I waited at home. I could tell Mom was terribly afraid that she might have been guilty of burning down the church.

Ten minutes later my father returned. He let out a relieved sigh and said, "Now I understand. The pot *was* on—burned empty and beginning to smoke."

And what, a half hour earlier, had waked us? The smoke alarm in our own—smoke-free—house.

—*Tracey Daniels*

Fleeing for Our Lives

Why did I snatch up such unusual things to take with me on that terrible night? When you're under pressure, you do strange—and mysterious—things.

And I was under terrible pressure.

Our whole family had lived under the threat of death for almost a year. We'd been afraid ever since Communists took over our country, Ethiopia, in September 1974. Our longtime emperor, Haile Selassie, had been arrested and sixty-two of the country's leading officials had been shot. Our land teemed with ruthless Marxists and fanatic radicals intent on eliminating people such as we: I was a government loyalist who had served as a senator in the emperor's parliament; my husband, Deme, was a prosperous businessman who had once headed several government departments for the emperor.

There was another reason our family was in peril. My husband and I were outspoken Christians.

Now it was the fourth day since we'd learned that our emperor had died. And with his death came a new wave of arrests. To save our lives, it seemed to us that our only hope was to flee south across the border into Kenya, a trip of some five hundred miles, leaving our home in Addis Ababa and all our possessions behind.

For an exorbitant sum we found a driver and a guide who would transport us in their ancient Land-Rover. It was a trip that seemed impossible, for we knew we'd have to detour via farm fields and river gorges to avoid police roadblocks, and cross forbidding terrain—yet we were ready to trust in God's promise: "But my God shall supply all your need according to his riches in glory by Christ Jesus" (Philippians 4:19).

We'd hoped to have a day or two to plan for our trip. But now, on August 31, 1975, we felt compelled to leave immediately. Later we learned that an order for our arrest was being processed in police headquarters that very day.

There wasn't a moment to spare. Since informers were everywhere, we pretended we were going on a picnic. I hurried our three sons who were still with us in Ethiopia, Lali, nine, Beté, fifteen, and Mickey, twenty-two, into the vehicle.

There was some fried chicken in the refrigerator; I had our cook pack it in a pan of aluminum foil and put it into a cooler. What else? We couldn't take too much in case we were stopped; it would look too suspicious.

Hurry, hurry! my heart whispered. I grabbed up four cans of tomato juice and a bottle of water and climbed into the vehicle. The driver started the motor.

"Wait!" I said. I dashed back into the house, wondering, *What am I doing?* A roll of cloth adhesive tape had been left on a chair. I stuffed it into my purse. And there on a shelf was a jar of Vaseline. I made sure we took that too.

"Marta, please!" my husband pleaded. I climbed back aboard, and at 8:00 P.M. we drove off into the night.

We held our breath as we passed police barricades. Then, as we drove through the dark countryside past sleeping villages, I grieved for my fellow countrymen. What would happen to them in the hard times ahead?

My melancholy thoughts were interrupted when the old Land-Rover broke down. The fuel pump had given out. But in the morning we found a mechanic to fix it.

Later, as we rested beneath some acacia trees, we ate the cold chicken and drank the tomato juice. I started to dispose of the aluminum foil pan and the empty juice cans, but something stopped me. Without knowing why, I thrust them back into the cooler.

Already far behind schedule, we pressed on that evening to the town of Arba Mench, a Marxist stronghold. We prayed our way through the crowded streets and were on our way out of town when Deme looked behind us.

A police car was chasing us!

Our driver accelerated and switched off our lights. We veered off the road into the bush, lurching over the rough terrain, swerving to miss boulders and trees. We had shaken off our pursuers! But in the bush a thorny tree branch had ripped open the protective canvas cover on the Land-Rover. Cold night air poured in around us.

"If only we had something to repair the canvas with," Deme muttered as we shivered in the cold.

"But we do!" I exclaimed, reaching into my purse for the cloth tape.

As we repaired the top, our driver said, "You were smart to think about bringing that with you."

"But I didn't think of it," I said. "The Lord made me pick it up."

He grunted. "You really think that Allah is interested in such little things?"

"The Lord is always watching over us," I answered softly.

On the third night we had to follow a dry riverbed to bypass a dangerous town. The Land-Rover groaned and squealed as it bounced off rocks. Then, with a terrible jolt, it lurched to a halt.

We climbed out to look and were instantly engulfed by a whining cloud of stinging insects. As we beat the air to ward them off, we discovered that a wheel had fallen off; its lug nuts had loosened and were lost in the dark forever. Deme suggested we take two lug nuts from each of the other wheels, and we used them to put the fallen wheel in place once again. But that was just the beginning of our wheel troubles.

Our next hurdle was the town of Yaballo, where the road crews were on the alert for escapees. There was a rise in the road before town, and we figured our best chance was to coast silently down the hill and through town just before dawn, when people would be sleeping their soundest.

Thank God, it worked.

Then we faced the most dangerous place of all—Mega, a city near the border, where all traffic was funneled through a police checkpoint. Deme, the driver and guide hoped they would look like a road crew. The boys and I hid on the floor in the rear of the Land-Rover. Slowly we drove past the police guard. Since most of the crews drove Land-Rovers, the police waved us on. Deme and I breathed a prayer of relief.

To avoid highway patrols, we again turned off the road and followed a dry riverbed. But just as we were beginning to breathe easier, the Land-Rover's rear slammed onto the gravel with a bone-jarring jolt. We climbed out to find that the back wheel had broken away from the axle. Deme examined it.

"Powder," he groaned. "The wheel bearings have been ground to powder."

Now escape looked hopeless.

We waited fitfully through the night. As the light rose over the rolling hills, I raised my hands. "Thank You, Lord, for watching over us," I said. "Thank You that we broke down here instead of in a town. Thank You for providing this day for us."

Deme knelt at the wheel.

"Can you fix it?" I asked.

He shook his head. "Not unless we had new wheel bearings or—" He jumped up. "Or we had something to fill up the space in place of the bearings."

He began rummaging through the truck, then opened the cooler. "This just might work!" he exclaimed. Taking the aluminum foil, he folded it into tight strips. Then, fitting them into the wheel, he said, "Marta, we need grease. Do you have any cosmetics? Any cold cream?"

I reached into my purse and held up the jar of Vaseline—the jar the Lord had prompted me to retrieve as we left.

By Friday noon, the fifth day of our flight, the Land-Rover limped slowly along. We'd had no water for a day and a half; our throats were parched and our tongues, swollen. That evening our vehicle shuddered and collapsed. The back wheel had fallen off again. The foil bearings had been chewed away.

Had we come this far, I wondered, *to die here in the midst of nowhere?*

Deme slipped down against the Land-Rover and, as if in prayer, sighed: "What do we have left? One wrench, half a jar of Vaseline, four empty tomato juice cans and seven people dying of thirst."

Suddenly he leaped up. "That's it," he exclaimed. "The tomato juice cans!"

As the sun rose on Saturday, Deme stomped the cans flat, shaped them into a metal tube around the wheel shaft and applied the last of the precious Vaseline.

By noon that day we faced the desert. Grim and foreboding, it undulated endlessly before us. Hour after hour we drove into charcoal-gray nothingness; even the sky had turned that sickly shade.

The Land-Rover's metal was searing hot. I looked anxiously at our son Beté. He was in a stupor, dehydrated.

"Deme, we must find water for Beté!"

My husband buried his face in his hands, then looked up to

heaven. Suddenly his face lit up: "There *is* water here. In the radiator. I saw the mechanic fill it with plain water."

I worried as we drained the steaming rust-brown water into our one remaining glass. I tried to strain it through a tissue, then handed the glass to Beté.

"Don't drink it," I cautioned. "Just rinse your mouth." He grabbed it and gulped it down. Mickey and Lali did the same. Their thirst was quenched—and the liquid didn't seem to harm them.

As we rode on into the blazing afternoon, we began to see hills in the distance. Then, near 6:00 P.M., we saw a cluster of houses ahead where a dozen handsome Kenyans stood waiting for us.

We had found sanctuary.

However, now we faced the unknown. Destitute, where would we go? What would we do? Moreover, as I glanced back at the gray desert, my heart cried out for the countrymen I had left behind.

For a moment, deep sadness for the past and fear of the future gripped me. Then I looked at Deme. He smiled and took my hand. I knew what he was thinking: We had the most valuable thing of all—our faith.

Surely God would do as much with that as He had done with a roll of tape, a piece of aluminum foil, four tomato juice cans and a jar of Vaseline.

—*Marta Gabre-Tsadick*

Gasoline Leak!

I was twenty-three years old that summer of 1944 during World War II and I'd just been promoted to flight engineer in our squadron. Our 62nd Troop Carrier Group was based in central Italy, but my plane and two other C–47s—Gooney Birds we called them—were sent up to southern France to ferry gasoline to General George Patton's tanks. In their great sweep across France, they had outdistanced their supply lines and were in desperate need of fuel.

One dawn after takeoff, I made my usual visit to the cargo area of our plane to see that everything was secure. An acrid smell hit my nostrils. One of the fifty–five–gallon barrels had sprung a leak and gasoline was spraying onto the floorboards!

"Oh, oh," I said out loud. "Trouble." The motors on that C–47 were set out on each wing only eight feet from the cabin. Tongues of flame four or five feet long trailed out of each exhaust stack.

I tore back to my compartment and grabbed some toothpicks. Maybe they would plug the leak. I tried one after the other. No good!

Desperate, I scrambled back to my compartment again. And then I remembered the eighteen-piece pack of chewing gum I'd bought the week before and left on my flight table.

God gave my jaws the power to chew eighteen pieces of gum for the eighteen successive plugs that the leak required until we landed safe and sound. But His greatest gift was getting me to buy that gum in the first place. You see, I never chew gum and that was the first pack of gum I'd bought in all the time I was overseas.

—*William Z. Whitehead*

Too Tired to Swim

When our sons, Chet and Jeff, were teenagers, they always celebrated the end of a long trip home to Florida by dashing out of the car and jumping into our swimming pool. It was the finishing touch to a journey—as much a family tradition as the prayers that started a trip. My wife, Catherine, our children and I never set out without first asking for God's protection from trip's beginning to trip's end.

One year before leaving Virginia, the family prayed together as usual, asking God to be especially close. We made the trip south without incident. But on arriving home, the boys failed to make their customary dash to the pool. "Too tired," they said.

In checking things around the house, I started to switch on

the underwater light that creates a beautiful glow in the pool. But the switch was already on the "on" position. *Odd,* I thought. *Well, I guess the bulb burned out.* But then a prickly feeling crept over me.

Immediately I taped the switch in the "off" position and made sure that no one was to enter the pool.

The next morning, I called an electrician, who checked the pool light carefully. "You've got an old, obsolete fixture here," he said. "Must've been here before you bought the place. Anyhow, water got into the light socket and shorted the circuit. Good thing nobody went swimming—they would have been electrocuted."

More than a good thing. For our family, it was one more example of how God touches our lives in a supernatural way when we seek His help.

—*Leonard E. LeSourd*

The Door

I slipped off my eyeglasses and smiled. I'd been watching my wife's sister and my namesake brother-in-law decorating their apartment. It was great sharing the holiday season with Barbara and Bob Kirkpatrick. My wife, Harriet, and I had faced a rather lonely Christmas in the snowy isolation of upstate New York that year, until we received the invitation to spend a vacation with the Kirkpatricks in Dallas. Their apartment was in the plush and modern Athena Complex. "There'll be plenty of room," Bob had promised.

So we came, just in time to trim the tree and help with other last-minute preparations. And the early morning hours of the day before Christmas Eve found Harriet and me sleeping soundly in the guest bedroom.

A scream from my brother-in-law woke us.

Still in our nightclothes, we opened the door to the living room. A glowing orange haze contrasted eerily with the darkness. Bob, sounding strangely distant, shouted something about a fire.

"We'll look for a fire hose!" I heard him call. Then I heard the metallic sound as he opened the steel door that led from the apartment to the outer corridor.

Attempting to follow his voice, Harriet and I bumped, then crawled aimlessly in the half-lit surroundings. "This is dangerous," I pointed out. "It's all strange—if we go out in the hallways, we might get lost. And we don't know where the smoke is coming from. Let's sit tight in the bedroom until we know what to do."

We were still huddled in the bedroom waiting for the Kirkpatricks' return when the electricity cut out minutes later.

"Don't worry, hon," I said, though I was also trembling. "I'll see what's happening."

I swung the door open and couldn't believe my eyes. Fire had already swept into the living room. The hot breath of flames flew at my face. It was all confusion. My first instinct was to grab Harriet's arm and attempt a run through the flames. But I hesitated. We could easily get hurt or lost in the smoky, unfamiliar corridors. "Lord, please help me make the right decision," I prayed.

Whatever choice I made would be fateful. Fourteen floors up, there would be no escape if we stayed in our bedroom. There was no exit from it: only one window, no terrace. Yet something, almost against reason, forced me to go back there, to slam the door behind us.

As our eyes grew accustomed to the darkness, Harriet saw the telephone on the night table. She sprang for the receiver and held it eagerly to her ear. Only gradually did she lower it.

"No dial tone," she choked finally. "The line is dead."

Her words were interrupted by a great crash and roar from the next room. We both gazed at the wall. It was as though some living evil lay beyond it, trying to force its way in.

Fearfully, we both began to pray without hope, without plan. We just asked, "God, please be with us." Even that did us good.

Our composure was better after praying. And now my mind was working. "God hasn't forgotten us—look, Harriet!" I said, gesturing with conviction at the doorway. "That's a steel door He gave us. Flames won't eat through steel. If we barricade it shut—and keep everything else good and damp—we should be able to keep out the flames a little while. Until help comes."

Feverishly, we set to work. Somehow, Harriet helped me shove a heavy wooden dresser against the door. Then we turned on the faucets in the bathroom that adjoined the bedroom. When the tub and sink overflowed we let the water soak the floor and carpet of our fifteen-by-thirteen-foot room. Meanwhile, we tore up towels, soaked them, and stopped up the ventilators where smoke was streaming in. As another precaution, I used my shoe to smash open the fastened window. December air whistling in gave us an odd chill despite the growing heat.

At the window, Harriet and I both yelled for help. But our cries were lost in the night air.

"O Lord, what do we do now?" I prayed.

For the first time, I noticed a plastic waste basket floating out from beneath the bathroom sink. "We'll use that to wet down the walls!" I exclaimed. Harriet nodded. Silently, we took turns from then on, splashing bucketfuls of water against the bedroom walls. At one point, we pulled the bedspread off and plunged it in the tub; we intended to hang it by the door for further protection. But we had to give up the idea when we found that even the two of us couldn't lift the heavy, sodden spread.

Harriet went to the closet farther along the wall from the door. She felt inside.

"This back wall is awfully hot!" she cried. So we splashed that with water, too.

At first, it was an activity of minutes. But the minutes added up, and stretched incredibly on. Soon we'd been trapped almost an hour. In our growing state of terror, we didn't talk much, to avoid the panicky sound of our own voices. Hopelessly, Harriet lay on the bed and silently covered herself with blankets during a rest period. *Maybe I can save her,* I thought, *if I tie enough bedsheets together and lower her through the window.* I mentioned the idea to Harriet.

She shook her head. "We're on the *fourteenth* floor. Besides," she added, "do you think I'd ever leave you?" She rose from the bed with new determination. "We'll stay; the door will keep the fire out of here, with God's help," she said.

The walls of the room were steamingly alive. Beyond them, popping and crashing noises told me that surrounding rooms—the living room, kitchen, and master bedroom—were furnaces now, incinerating their contents. *God,* I prayed, *will the floors be next? Or these walls?* But, like Harriet, my thoughts returned like a magnet to the door. Unreasonably, it seemed to symbolize safety from the holocaust around us. "Yes, we can stay safe in here, as long as we keep wetting things down and waiting for help," I said. Water splashed on the walls sizzled hotly now. If the bedroom overheated much more, I knew it could burst into flames. Helplessly, I located a jewelry box and hurled it to the pavement far below our window. But this was a back street. The crowds of evacuees from the building had assembled behind fire lines forming on a main street in front of the building.

"They don't know we're up here," Harriet moaned. "We're lost."

Heartsick, I held her in my arms. For the first time, I believed it was over, too. We crouched as drifting smoke filled the upper part of the room. But we resolved to keep splashing the water. And then, a final disaster. Harriet slipped and fell on the wet bathroom floor. Bones in her ankle were either broken or badly dislocated. She could hardly move.

When I saw the sickening swelling of Harriet's leg, I no longer thought of escape. Everything now depended on God's protection. The fire sounded like some hellish whirlwind just beyond the steel door; I remember thinking that it was the only thing that kept death away. No more talking—we wrapped in wet blankets, we held each other in our arms. No more talking—we just silently prayed. An odd thought occurred to me then. After coming all the way to Texas to avoid a "lonely" Christmas—at a moment like this—we'd found that all we needed for comfort was to be together.

Then suddenly, amid the deep roar of the flames, we heard an ominous new sound. Like thunder.

Harriet recognized it first. "It's water . . . water! Firemen's hoses!"

We screamed together. In a few moments our rescuers were pounding at the bedroom door. Gratefully, we shoved the heavy dresser aside and collapsed into their arms. I have only the dimmest recollection of the tortuous route that we followed, in and out of black rooms and dark hallways and, finally, outside.

It was ended. But there was an aftermath.

Next day, while Harriet rested her injuries (her ankle was treated for fractures) I accompanied a fire marshal—and my brother-in-law, Bob—back to the fourteenth floor of the Athena to survey the scene of the blaze.

"When Barb and I came back after looking for a fire hose and saw all those flames, we were sure you'd left already," Bob had explained. "Only later, when we couldn't find you on the street, did we start to really worry. A fireman told us, 'There's no way anybody could be alive up there.' "

The near-accuracy of that statement made my stomach feel queasy when I saw the apartment again. The walls were charcoal. Heat generated by the fire had been so intense that it had consumed everything in the room. Where the Christmas tree had been, where sofas and chairs and tables had stood—there was now only ash scattered on the floor. Even the porcelain fixtures were gone.

Only the room where Harriet and I had withstood the siege was nearly intact. I pointed to the blackened door.

"That steel door," I began. "It saved . . ."

My voice broke off. I shook uncontrollably as I watched the fire marshal swing the door open, flaking dark chips off the outside. The door that had looked like solid steel was hollow—and it was *made of wood!*

I thought about the conviction I'd held the terrible night before: Keep splashing water around and stay behind the safety of that door. There had to be a reason that that flimsy door had not burned through. And there was only one answer for Harriet and me.

Someone Whose protection was more powerful than steel had been with us that night.

—*Robert L. Daugherty*

Prayer

Lord, be Thou within me, to strengthen me;
Without me, to keep me;
Above me, to protect me;
Beneath me, to uphold me;
Before me, to direct me;
Behind me, keep me from straying;
Round about me, to defend me.
Blessed be Thou, our Father, for ever and ever.
—*Lancelot Andrewes*

GOD
HEALS

Bless the Lord, O my soul . . .
who forgiveth all thine iniquities;
who healeth all thy diseases;
who redeemeth thy life from destruction.
                    —Psalm 103:2–3

God is the ultimate healer, as these stories show. But we have a part to play, too. By our faith, we put ourselves in God's healing hands. By focusing on the sufferings of Christ, we are enabled to move out of our suffering. By forgiving others and accepting God's forgiveness, we free our spirits to receive God's loving help.

These stories do not answer the question why some people are healed and others aren't. But they do show how closely linked our bodies and our spirits are. And they point us in the direction of faith and surrender—the need to put ourselves in tune with God and His will for us. Many of the people who came to Jesus for healing and received their health from Him were told, "Your faith has saved you." For a short space of time their attention was focused outside themselves—on Jesus and His power.

To some people God gives the gift of healing (see 1 Corinthians 12:9). And though not everyone receives this gift from the Holy Spirit, we can offer ourselves in prayer for the sufferings of others. Then, like one young woman who for a little while took on the paralysis of a co-worker and the next morning found that the other woman had been healed, we too may receive a miracle.

Good Friday in the Garden

"Freda, this looks like a good day to plant those seeds," my husband, John, said as he left for his barbershop. That afternoon, in the sunshine's warmth, I knelt in the garden planting sweet-pea seeds. It was Good Friday, and the hour when most people in town were at church.

I was still recovering from a serious operation. The doctor didn't think I would walk again. I could get around only with the aid of a walker, and I felt slow, awkward, frustrated. My recovery seemed far away.

"Why *Good* Friday?" I wondered. For Jesus it had been a day of sadness, pain.

Crawling slowly on my knees, I poked a finger into the earth, dropped in a seed, then covered it. *Soon shoots will be popping through the spring snow,* I told myself. I pictured them, could almost smell their fragrance.

In my garden I felt very near to God. I thought of Christ praying in the Garden of Gethsemane. And as I struggled on my knees, my thoughts traveled with Jesus to His trial, then to Golgotha, where He suffered on the cross. I remembered His cry, "It is finished."

I, too, had suffered, had lingered near death after brain surgery. Only my faith and my family had sustained me.

Working in the soil, I felt at peace, and strengthened. Tucking in the last seed, I stood and gazed proudly at my neat row. "Well, it's finished."

My thoughts remained on Good Friday as I walked to the house. At the porch, I glanced back at my garden.

Then I saw, standing among the rows . . . "My walker!" I gasped. I had walked without it. And I haven't needed it since.

—*Freda Creager*

Petition in Faith

I am empty, Lord: fill me;
Sick with sorrow: heal me;
Blinded by worldly ways: show me;
I rush into foolishness, Lord: slow me.

Like an earthly garden, Lord, I need You to tend
    me;
Like a garment worn and torn, mend me;
Like an empty cup, fill me till I overflow
With Your loving goodness, Lord,
So all the world may know:

That I was empty, Lord, and You filled me;
Sick with sorrow, yet You healed me;
Blinded with worldly ways, until You came to
    show me
That the only way to peace, dear Lord, is
To know Thee.

                                   —*Terry Tucker Francis*

Angel Cups

Some years ago I worked in a small TV station in California
that was owned and operated by a large parent station two
hundred miles away. My job was to write copy for local com-
mercials and that particular year, as the Christmas season advanced, the repetition of writing "buy this" and "buy that" got
me down. It was the strongest dose of the wrong side of
Christmas I had ever experienced.

One night at home I mulled over the copy I had written that
day and there, all alone, I began to talk to God. "O Lord," I
said, "if only there was something in my job about a Christmas
gift you didn't have to buy, something with no strings, no
profits, no angles, no ten percent down. Just for love." For
several days this yearning deepened within me.

Christmas Eve afternoon we had a quiet employees' party in the office kitchen. We were all standing together in a little knot of self-conscious conviviality when Mr. Barstow, down from the parent station, passed out a brightly wrapped present to each of us—the same gift for everyone, a cheery coffee mug with an amusing little angel face on it and the employee's name labeled in gold beneath. When I opened mine I noticed the mistake immediately. The name "Anna" was on my cup.

"They've given you the wrong one," Mr. Barstow said apologetically. "That's for one of the girls in bookkeeping back in the home office. And she probably has yours. Listen, I'll take it back with me now and I'll have yours shipped to you right away."

It seemed to me that Mr. Barstow was overly concerned about the matter. "That's too much trouble," I protested. "I don't mind having Anna's if she doesn't mind having mine."

"No, I want to straighten it out. It's important. Anna's in the hospital."

"What's the matter?" Janet, our traffic-log girl, asked.

"She's paralyzed," Mr. Barstow told us. He didn't know the medical details, but Anna was in serious condition.

The party picked up again and we all had coffee in the new cups. Yet, I hesitated. I felt superstitious about drinking from Anna's cup. After a few sips I put it down.

When I went to bed that Christmas Eve, I easily fell asleep. It had been a hectic day. But in the middle of the night I awakened suddenly, sharply, to one of the strangest experiences of my life. As I lay there fully awake, an inexplicable feeling of grief washed over me. I did not know why or what caused it, but tears started rolling down my cheeks and, as I tried to take my hands to wipe them away, I found to my shock that my arms would not move. I could not lift them.

In a single wave of remembrance, I recalled the angel cup. Anna's cup. Now I wept uncontrollably. "God," I prayed out loud, and the words seemed to come not so much from me as from an outside force, "help her!" Again I tried to raise my arms. They were glued to my sides. "Look, look, God, that's the way it is with Anna. She can't even raise her arms to pray. Help her."

More and more I went on. I was praying in a fashion unlike

myself, praying outside my own efforts, like a fountain pouring
from an unknown source. Part of me seemingly stood aside,
watching and listening in amazement. Gradually then, my
arms lost their heaviness and slowly I found I could raise them,
up, up, up. How good it felt! Now my prayer became one of
thanksgiving, and as suddenly as it had come, the grief left me.
The tears stopped. I fell asleep.

I was off Christmas Day, but when I returned to the office
it fell my lot to take the regular afternoon hot-line phone call
from the parent studio. My little office was filled with people.
The six o'clock news announcer was checking his copy. The
manager was shouting at the cameraman to use the No. 2
camera for the jewelry commercial due on the screen in ten
minutes. One of the engineers stood by my desk ready to talk
as soon as I had finished. But just before I relinquished the
phone, I asked, "How is Anna?"

"She's better. Just all of a sudden in the early hours of
Christmas she could move her arms and legs again. It—well—
it was really strange."

"How wonderful," I said quietly, wildly excited inside.

"Wasn't it a marvelous Christmas gift for her!"

"Yes. What a marvelous Christmas gift," I said—and surrounded by all the noisy pressure and push of the office, a small
center of silence glowed inside me as I gave the phone over
to the impatient engineer.

—*Lucy Meyer*

The Woman from Nowhere

My preschooler son Marc and I were shopping in a large
department store. On our way down to the main floor, Marc
hopped on the escalator. I followed. Suddenly Marc screamed.
I'd never heard a sound like that before. "Mama! My foot!"

Marc's right foot was wedged between the side of the moving step and the escalator's wall. His body was twisted toward
me. He screamed again. The escalator continued downward.

In the panic of the moment, the danger at the bottom of the

escalator flashed before me, the thought of the foot being severed—

"Turn off the escalator!" I screamed. "Somebody help!" And then, "Oh, dear God, dear God, help us! Help us!"

Several people at the base of the escalator began a flurry of activity. The escalator stopped! Someone had pressed an emergency button at the bottom of the steps.

Thank You, Father, I prayed.

Marc clutched my arm and cried while I struggled to get a better look at his foot. A chill raced up my spine when I saw the tiny space in which his foot was trapped. It looked no more than a quarter of an inch wide. All I could see of his foot was his heel. The rest had disappeared into the jaws of the machine.

"Someone call the fire department!" I shouted.

Marc looked up at me desperately. "Mama," he said, "pray!"

I crouched next to him, holding him. I prayed. For a moment he quieted. Soon, though, he began crying again. "Daddy! Daddy!" he called out. I shouted out our business phone number, hoping someone would call my husband.

The two of us sat waiting. Marc cried. I patted his head. As the minutes passed I could see dark images of crutches and wheelchairs. I had always taken for granted that our little son would grow up playing baseball and soccer, running on strong legs and sturdy feet. Now, nothing seemed certain.

My prayers were as scattered as my feelings, and I searched my memory for a Bible verse to hold on to.

"And we know that all things work together for good to them that love God, to them who are the called according to his purpose" (Romans 8:28). This was one of the few verses I had memorized.

"You promised, Lord!" I cried. "And we know that all things . . ." Over and over I said that verse. ". . . called according to his purpose."

Marc looked up at me and said, "Mama, my bones feel broken and bleedy."

I clutched his blond head tighter to me, but now it was I who was feeling faint. *I can't faint, Lord,* I prayed. *Marc needs me—O Lord, I know You're here! Where? Help me!*

At that moment I felt warm soft arms enfolding me from behind. A woman's soothing voice said quietly in my ear, "Jesus is here, Jesus is here."

The woman had come down the escalator and sat on the step above me. She gently rocked me from side to side, surrounding my shaking body with a calm embrace. "Tell your son his foot is all right," she said in my ear. There was an assurance in her voice.

"Marc," I said into his ear. "Your foot is all right."

"Tell him you'll buy him a new pair of shoes—whatever kind he wants."

"I'll buy you a new pair of shoes. Any kind you like."

Marc's crying stopped. "Cowboy boots? Like Daddy's?" We were talking about new shoes—new shoes for two healthy feet! For the first time since the ordeal began, I felt hope. Maybe, just maybe, his foot really would be all right.

"Tell him there are no broken bones," she said.

I did.

The firemen arrived. Two men with crowbars pried the step away from the escalator wall, freeing Marc's foot at last. His shoe was in tatters. It took all my courage to watch as the men pulled the shredded sock off Marc's foot, but when they did, they revealed a red, bruised, but whole foot.

I turned to share my joy with my wonderful friend, but all I saw was her leg as she turned the corner at the top of the escalator. I never even saw her face.

My husband, Craig, arrived just as the firemen were setting Marc down on the floor. He was still sobbing, but he could wiggle his toes. Later, X rays confirmed what I already knew: no broken bones, only bruises and swelling.

To this day I do not know who the woman who helped me was, who knew that Jesus was there with us, who knew that the Lord keeps His promises.

Many people have suggested that the woman was an angel of the Lord. I can't be sure about that, but of this I am certain: She was heaven-sent.

—*Laura Z. Sowers*

Three Months in His Presence

When friends ask how I first discovered that my hands have been given a ministry of healing, I'm sure they don't expect to hear the kind of story that I am about to set down. Apparently the fact that I am a suburban housewife who saves grocery stamps and has to watch her weight seems a poor beginning to a story of divine intervention.

It started the year my father entered the tuberculosis sanitarium in Tampa, Florida. We had long since given up hope. He was too old for an operation and we had seen the X rays. The last thing on earth that would have occurred to any of us—Mother or my sister or me—was to ask God to step in and change medical facts.

And yet my husband, Ed, and I were active church members. As a banker, Ed was head of fund-raising, our two children went to Sunday school and I belonged to all the usual groups. We were, in short, typical, civic-minded churchgoers. Which is why the tears, when they began, caused us so much embarrassment.

It was in October, driving home from a PTA meeting, that I suddenly began to cry. I was in charge of the Halloween carnival that year, and at the meeting there had been some criticism of the plans. When I was still crying at bedtime, Ed put his arms around me and said, "Honey, all the carnivals in the world aren't that important."

But it wasn't the carnival. Even as I cried I knew that those tears were for something far bigger. I cried myself to sleep and in the morning, as soon as I opened my eyes, the tears started again. I choked them back while I fixed breakfast. But as soon as Ed and the children left, I burst into tears again.

This incredible state of affairs lasted four days. I took to wearing dark glasses even in the house so that my family would not guess how constantly I was crying. I was sure I was having a nervous breakdown.

It was on the morning of the fourth day, after Ed and the children had left, that a curious change took place. I saw nothing. I heard nothing. Yet all at once there was power in the air around me. The atmosphere itself seemed to hum and crackle as though I stood in the center of a vast electrical storm.

As I try to put it into words it sounds fantastic, but at the time there was no sense that something beyond the possible was taking place.

I had sunk into the high-backed chair in the living room when suddenly through the window I saw the eastern horizon. Trees and houses stood between me and it, but I seemed to see right beyond to the place where earth and sky came together. And there, where they met, was a ball of light.

The light was moving, traveling toward me with amazing speed. It appeared white, yet from it poured all the colors I had ever seen.

And then it was beside me. Although it seemed impossible that anything with such energy could hold still, it took a position at my right shoulder and there it stayed. And as I stared, I started to smile. I smiled because He was smiling at me. For I now saw that it was not light, but a face.

How can I put into words the most beautiful countenance I have ever seen? "He is perfect" was the first thought that came. His forehead was high, His eyes exceptionally large. But I could never fix the color of His eyes any more than I could the color of the sea.

More, much more, than individual features was the overwhelming impression of life—unhampered life, life so brimming over with power and freedom that all living things I had seen till then seemed lumps of clay by comparison.

Not for a moment did I hesitate to call this Life at my side Jesus. And two things about Him struck me most. The first was His humor. I was astonished to see Him often break into outright laughter. And the second was His utter lack of condemnation. That He knew me down to my very marrow—knew all the stupid, cruel, silly things I had ever done—I realized at once. But I also saw that none of those things, or anything I would ever do, could alter the absolute caring, the unconditional love, that I saw in those eyes.

I could not grasp it. It was too immense a fact. I felt that if I gazed at Him for a thousand years I could not realize it all.

I did not have a thousand years; I had three months. For as long as that, the face of Jesus stayed beside me, never fading, never withdrawing. Many times I tried to tell someone else what I saw but the words would never come. And meanwhile

I carried on with my tasks—meals and shopping and the PTA with its carnival—but effortlessly, scarcely knowing I was doing them, so fixed were my thoughts on Him.

At the same time, I had never seemed so aware of other people. How this was possible when my mind was full of Him alone I don't know, but it was true. My husband, especially. Far from feeling that a third person had entered our marriage, I felt that Christ *was* the marriage, as though all along He had been the force drawing us together.

And the Bible! All, at once I couldn't read enough of it. It was like tearing open a letter from someone who had known this Presence as a flesh-and-blood person, full of just the kind of specific details I longed to hear. Certain passages in particular had a strange effect on me. When the Bible described Jesus' healing someone, the actual print on the page seemed to burn. The hand that touched it tingled as if I had touched an electric current.

And then one afternoon before the children got home, I was sitting, just looking at Him, when all of a sudden, in a patch of sunlight on the wall, appeared the X ray of my father's chest. It was all scar tissue and cavities. Then as I watched, a white mist moved slowly up the wall. When it passed the diseased tissue, there appeared on my wall a picture of a healthy lung.

"Then Dad's well!" I said aloud, and at that the Person at my side burst into peal after peal of joyous laughter, which said that wholeness was always God's way.

I thought my heart would burst as I waited for the next Wednesday's X ray. I enjoyed the scene in my mind again and again, imagining the ring of the telephone and Mother's voice stammering with excitement, "Darling—the most amazing— the most glorious—"

But when Mother called, her voice was flat. "The most annoying thing, Virginia. They got the slides mixed up! Poor Dad's got to go back for X rays tomorrow. Why, they sent down pictures of someone who never even had TB . . . !"

But, of course, the next day's X rays showed no sign of disease either; Dad was healed and lived out his long life in thanksgiving to God.

And it was Dad's healing that convinced me I must try to

describe the indescribable that had happened to me. I went to an elderly pastor whom I had known a long time. To my astonishment he understood me at once. He gave me some books that described fairly similar things.

Then he said the words I have wished unsaid so many, many times. "Don't be surprised, Virginia, if the vision fades after a time. They usually do, you know."

Fade! I thought, as I drove home with that joyous Presence beside me. *Oh, it can't, it mustn't!* For the first time in the whole unbelievable experience my attention veered from Him to myself. And in that instant the vision was diminished, it actually disappeared for a second or two, though right away the radiant face was beside me again.

But the damage was done. The seed of self-concern was sown. The bright Presence would sometimes be missing for an hour or more. The more worried I got, the more self-centered I grew. What have I done? What will I do without Him? When He did return there would be no accusation in His eyes, just a tremendous compassion, as though He realized how difficult it had become for me to see Him.

At last all that was left of this experience was the strange tingling in my hands as I read the Bible stories of healing. One day I was visiting a friend in the hospital. She was hemorrhaging and in pain. On an impulse I reached out and touched her. My hand began to burn just as it did during the Bible reading. My friend gave a little sigh of comfort and fell asleep. When the doctor examined her, he found that the hemorrhaging had stopped.

Over the next eight years there were dozens, scores of experiences of that kind, all as inexplicable as the first. And yet for me they were still years of emptiness and waiting. "I will always be with you," He had said when I last saw Him.

"But how will I know if I can't see You?" I called to Him, for He had seemed so far away.

"You will see Me," He said, and then He was gone.

But the years went by and the vision had not come back. And then one day, while speaking to a church group, I saw those love-lit eyes smiling once again into mine. I looked again. The eyes belonged to a lady in the second row. Sud-

denly the room was full of Him; He was in the eyes of everyone there. "You will see Me . . ."

I used to wonder what would have happened if the old
pastor had never spoken of the vision's fading. Might I have
had it forever? I think not. I think that the days when Jesus was
real to my eyes were the days of the "childhood" of my faith,
the joyous, effortless time of discovery. But I do not think He
lets it stay that way.

He didn't for His first disciples; He doesn't for us today. He
gives us a glimpse only. Perhaps He let me look so long
because I am slow to learn. But, finally, He takes away all
sensory clues. He is bigger than our eyes and ears can make
Him, so He gives us instead the eyes of faith, and every human
being in which to discover His face.

—*Virginia Lively*

The Anonymous Caller

In 1977 I was in a Bloomington, Indiana, hospital with throat
cancer. My doctor had told me frankly that the prognosis was
not good. He talked to me calmly about my making a will and
other "practical" arrangements.

My speaking voice was reduced to a scratchy whisper. I
couldn't bring myself even to try to talk to anyone about my
situation. All I could do was what I'd done all my life when
scared or worried—read my Bible and talk to Jesus.

Later, when the phone beside my bed rang, I didn't recognize the caller's voice. "I was praying and reading my Bible,"
the woman said, "and the name 'Sandy Brown' appeared on
the page."

One of those cranks, I thought. But she'd mentioned my
maiden name. How could she know that? As I hesitated, her
voice continued. "Your hospital phone number also appeared
in my Bible. When your minister comes in today and prays,
you'll be healed." *Click.* She was gone.

My minister, Tom Calk, did visit me that afternoon. Just as

he was about to leave—without offering a prayer—I found myself grasping his hand.

"Tom, please pray for me."

He prayed. I began gasping as though something were being pushed down my throat. I was coughing, choking, swallowing constantly. Finally I was able to clear my throat.

"Are you *okay?*" Tom asked, anxiously.

"Yes, I think I'll be fine," I said. And my voice was normal.

Subsequently I had five chemotherapy treatments and three months later tests showed me cancer-free. I still am. And I've never heard from my anonymous caller again.

—*Sandy Drummond*

I Saw the Hand of God Move

I've always believed in God. But over the years my beliefs about Who God is—and what He can do—have changed. It wasn't until my son was gravely ill that I learned you can believe in God and yet not know Him at all.

Know. Knowledge. Logic. When I was younger, those were the words I wanted to live by. As a child I contracted scarlet fever, and this illness ruled out my ever playing sports or roughhousing around. The only real adventures I could go on were adventures of the mind. I read books with a vengeance—Great Books of the Western World, and the volumes of Will and Ariel Durant, and literally thousands more—and out of my reading I formed my strongest beliefs. I believed in logic, in the mind's ability to put all creation into neat, rational categories.

At the same time I was growing up in a strongly Christian family, and so I believed in God. But I insisted—and my insistence caused a lot of arguments—that God Himself was also a Being bound by logic and His own natural laws. I guess I pictured God as a great scientist. Miracles? No, God couldn't and wouldn't break laws in that way. When my family told me that Christianity means faith in a loving, miracle-working God,

I turned away and went looking for other religions—ones that respected the rational mind above all.

As I became a man, my belief in rationality helped me in my career. I became a salesman for the Bell System, and when I needed to formulate sales strategies and targets, logic unlocked a lot of doors on the way to success.

But other doors seemed to be closed. I felt dry, spiritually empty and anxious. I tried meditation, ESP and so on, but the emptiness increased to despair.

In utter defeat, I turned to God in prayer. His Spirit answered with, "I don't simply want belief that I exist. I want you, your will, your life, your dreams, your goals, your very being. And I want your faith, faith that I am sufficient for all your needs." My despair overcame my logic and I yielded all to Him. But just saying you have faith is not the same as having it. In my mind, I still had God in a box.

Maybe that's why I never thought to pray when my oldest son, Frank, came home from first grade one day and said he didn't feel well. What would God care about stomach flu?

A doctor whom my wife Janice and I had consulted wasn't very alarmed about Frank's illness at first. "It's really not too serious," the doctor assured us, "just a bad case of the flu complicated by a little acidosis. Give him this medicine and in a few days he'll be fine."

But Frank wasn't fine, not at all. The medicine worked for a day or so, but then his symptoms—the gagging, choking and vomiting—came back more violently. His small, six-year-old frame was bathed in sweat and racked with convulsions. We checked him into the local hospital for further testing, but later in the evening our doctor said the original diagnosis was correct. "He's just got a real bad case of it," we were told.

I went to work the next day fully expecting to take Frank and Janice home that night, but when I stopped at the hospital to pick them up, our doctor was there to meet me. "I'd like to have a word with you two," he said, showing Janice and me into a private room.

"A problem, Doctor?" I asked.

"Further testing has shown our previous diagnosis was incorrect. We think your son has acute nephritis. It's a terminal kidney disease . . ." He paused, and I could feel the blood running from my face. "But we've found that in children there's a good chance of recovery. Your son has a ninety percent chance of being as good as new."

But by ten o'clock the next morning the news was worse. Sometime during the night, Frank's kidneys had failed. Janice and I rushed to the hospital again.

"X rays show Frank's kidneys are so badly infected that no fluid will pass through them," we were told. "The odds aren't in his favor anymore. If those kidneys don't start working within forty-eight hours, I'm afraid your son will die."

I looked at Janice, watching the tears well in her eyes as a huge lump formed in my throat. I took her hand in mine and slowly we walked back to Frank's room. We were too shocked, too upset to even talk. All afternoon we sat at Frank's bedside, watching, stroking his matted blond hair, wiping his damp forehead. The stillness of the room was broken only by the beeps and blips of the machines monitoring little Frank's condition. Specialists would occasionally come, adjust a few tubes, make some marks on Frank's chart, and then silently go. I searched their eyes for an answer, for some glimmer of hope, and got nothing. When our minister came to pray for our son, I could only cry in desperation.

Late that evening, after Frank was asleep, we went home. Friends were waiting with a hot meal, words of encouragement and news of a vast prayer chain they had begun. And for a fleeting moment, I thought I saw in Janice's eyes the spark of hope that I had been looking for from the doctors all afternoon.

By the following morning, that spark of hope had ignited a flame of confidence in Janice. "I turned Frank's life over to God last night," she told me excitedly, before we were even out of bed. "I feel a real peace about what's going to happen, that God's will is going to be done."

"God's will?" I said angrily. "What kind of God makes little boys get sick? He doesn't care!" And I rolled over. Peace? God's will? No, little Frank would need more than that to get well.

But my anger didn't stop me from trying to reason with God. All that morning, while Janice kept a hospital vigil, I begged and pleaded and screamed at God, daring Him to disprove my skepticism, trying to goad Him into action.

"Who do You think You are?" I shouted once. "Why are You doing this to my son? He's only six! Everybody says You're such a loving God—why don't You show it?" I yelled until I was exhausted. Finally, convinced my arguments were falling on deaf ears, I took our other children to a neighbor and headed to the hospital, thinking this might be the last time I'd see my son alive.

I never arrived; at least, a part of me didn't. In the car on the way, this Higher Being, this remote Power, this unjust God, spoke to me through His Spirit. I felt His presence, soothing my still-hot anger. And I heard His voice, gentle, reassuring. He reminded me that I had made a commitment to Him, that I had promised to trust Him with my life, my all. And He had promised to take care of me, in all circumstances. "Take Me out of the box you've put Me in," He said, "and let Me work." By the time I parked the car, my heart was beating wildly. I sat for a few moments longer, and uttered but two words in reply to all that had happened: "Forgive me."

By the time I reached Frank's room, I knew what I needed to do as clearly as if someone had given me written instructions. There had been no change in Frank's condition, so I sent Janice home to get some rest. Then I walked over to Frank's bed. Placing shaking hands on where I thought his kidneys should be, I prayed as I never believed I would ever pray. "God, forgive me for my ego, for trying to make You what I want You to be. If You will, heal my son, and if You won't, that's all right too. I'll trust You. But, please, do either right now, I pray in Christ's name. Amen."

That was all. There were no lightning flashes, no glows, no surges of emotion like the rushing wind, only the *blip-blip-blip* of monitors. I calmly sat down in a chair, picked up a magazine, and began to wait for God's answer. There was only one difference. For the first time in my life, I knew I was going to get one.

Within moments my eyes were drawn from the magazine to a catheter tube leading from Frank's frail-looking body. That tube was supposed to drain fluid from his kidneys, but for nearly two days it had been perfectly dry, meaning Frank's kidneys weren't working at all. But when I looked closely at the top of the tube, I saw a small drop of clear fluid forming. Ever so slowly it expanded, like a drop of water forming on the head of a leaky faucet, until it became heavy enough to run down the tube and into the collecting jar.

This was the most wonderful thing I had ever seen—the hand of God, working. I watched the tube, transfixed, fully expecting to see another drop of fluid form. In about two minutes, I did. Soon, the drops were coming regularly, about a minute apart. With every drip, I could hear God saying to me, "I am, and I care."

When the nurse came in on her regular half-hour rounds, she could barely contain her excitement. "Do you see this, do you see this?" she shouted, pointing to the collecting jar. "Do you know that this is more fluid than your son has excreted in the past forty-eight hours combined." She grabbed the catheter and raised it, saying she wanted to get every drop, then rushed off.

Within minutes she was back. Grabbing a chair, she sat down next to me and, excitedly, we watched drops of fluid run down the tube. We were both awed at what was happening; for half an hour we murmured only short sentences. "Isn't God good?" she asked me once, and I nodded. When she finally got up to call the doctor, I went to call Janice.

An hour and a half later one of the specialists assigned to Frank's case arrived. Taking one look at the collector, he told us that it was a false alarm, that the fluid was too clear. Anything coming from a kidney as infected as Frank's was would be rust-colored and filled with pus. No, he said, the fluid had to be coming from somewhere else. But I knew—Frank was well again.

By the next morning more than five hundred centimeters of the clear fluid had passed into the collector, and it continued as the doctors ran tests and X rays to try to determine its origin. Finally, two days later, our doctor called us into his office.

"Joe, Janice, I think we've been privileged to witness an act of God. All the X rays taken in the last two days not only show no kidney infection, they show no sign that there was ever an infection. Frank's blood pressure and blood poison levels have also dropped suddenly . . . It is a definite miracle."

And this time I wasn't about to argue. At last I fully believed in a God Whose love knows no bounds . . . not the bounds of logic, not the hold of natural laws. *Faith.* That's what I now had . . . that and the knowledge that one's belief in God is essentially hollow if the belief isn't founded on faith.

—*Joe Stevenson*

"With the Lord There Is Mercy"

After a welding torch accident, I lay in Intensive Care with eighty percent of my body burned. But I felt the presence of God, and I knew I was not going to die. I felt protected by the prayers of my family and friends. I was buoyed by an ecumenical prayer chain, by the children's Sunday school class that made get-well cards, by the high school athletes who raised money for my hospital bills.

Then, as I began to improve, some discomforting thoughts gradually entered my mind. "Why do I deserve all this love?" I asked myself. "I've made a lot of mistakes. I've done things I'm ashamed of."

Suddenly I slipped into a relapse. My temperature climbed and I stopped making progress. In my feelings of guilt, I had stopped calling on God. Then one night—to my surprise—I found myself asking a nurse to read to me from the Bible.

She picked up my Bible and began to read from it at random. "Out of the depths have I cried unto thee, O Lord."

It was Psalm 130—the perfect prayer for a man who felt unworthy!

"If thou, Lord, shouldest mark iniquities, O Lord, who shall stand? But there is forgiveness with thee . . . for with the Lord there is mercy. . . ."

When she finished, she routinely took my temperature. But the look on her face when she read the thermometer was not at all routine. "It's down," she said. "You're better!"

What strange events! God had saved my life; then I'd let my

guilt get in the way of His healing power. But He wouldn't have it! He used a nurse and a Scripture verse to unburden my mind so He could finish healing my body—completely.

—David Snitker

"I'm God's Property"

The headaches and exhaustion that had plagued me for weeks were getting worse. Finally a specialist diagnosed my problem as hemolysis—the destruction of the red blood cells. The type I had was fatal—usually in a matter of months. And I was only forty-five, with a husband and three children to care for.

"Your blood cells are bursting like little balloons," doctors told me. "But we still don't know the reason. Your condition is so advanced that any treatments or drugs are just too risky. All we can do is *wait.*"

Alone in a hospital room, I was nauseous with fear. I was especially concerned for my little daughter Marcia. She was my Down's syndrome child; how would she get along?

Marcia! Whenever she was frightened, she'd call out: "Devil, take your hands off me! I'm God's property!" She'd heard that on TV. We'd always smiled at her simple trust. Yet now I wondered: Did I have enough faith to say those words—and *mean* them? With unusual boldness, I said, "Satan, take your hands off me! I'm God's child and I won't die till He's through with me!"

Almost immediately, the nausea left. I felt Christ's presence!

I went home, but returned to the hospital three times a week for blood tests. By the second visit, the doctor reported that my blood count had climbed three points. "What's happening?" he asked, bewildered.

Five months later—without drugs or treatment of any kind—my blood count was normal. There was no trace of the hemolysis. The doctors were astounded.

But I wasn't, and today I often take Marcia in my arms, hold her tight and say, "Devil, get away! We're *both* God's property!"

—Joanna Daniel

The Cure

Paco and I stared at each other through an invisible wall of mounting tension. "I'm not leaving," I said flatly. "I'm just too sick to travel."

Paco rolled his eyes upward, calling on his Guatemalan gods to witness the unreasonableness of the American tourist lady. "But señora," he protested for the fifteenth time, "the down-river boat isn't due until another two days. Perhaps by then . . ."

I closed my red-rimmed, watery eyes, hoping to close off the conversation. The cold in my head made it feel three sizes too big. My throat was on fire, and every shred of my body ached.

"Perhaps by then . . ." I was wallowing in self-pity, "perhaps by then I may be dead!"

Immediately I was sorry. After all, I was virtually an intruder in this small, little-known village in the far upper reaches of Guatemala. A week ago I had traveled here, first by rickety, hedgehopping jungle airline, then by Jeep, and finally by boat, in order to photograph an obscure, old Mayan temple ruin.

From the village of a hundred and fifty or so inhabitants, I had selected Paco's as the most promising of primitive guest facilities. He had been happy to receive me then, since I was his only customer. Shortly afterward, however, he had word that a boatload of twelve students from a U.S. university would be arriving to study the same site, on the very day I was scheduled to leave. Since they would be staying for six weeks, and he could rent his room to as many as three students, it was a windfall he and his family could ill-afford to lose.

I stifled my conscience telling me I was being selfish proposing to wait for the following boat—just long enough for all the students to get settled elsewhere. After all, I reminded myself, of all the bad colds I'd had, this one was undoubtedly the most painful and miserable. I couldn't afford to take chances by stirring about too soon.

But if I was desperate, so was Paco. He played his trump card. "There's only one thing left to do," he announced with finality. "I'll have to call on the *curadera.*"

"Oh-h-h no!" I wheezed. "No lady witch doctors!" Then again, empathizing with his situation, I softened. "You see, I am a Christian. Her magic wouldn't work on me." But we were both talking at once, neither listening to the other. *At least I owe him the courtesy of a hearing,* I told myself.

". . . and she is a very old woman," he was saying, "older than almost any of us. For most of our lives she has kept sickness and bad luck from our village with the corn magic handed down from the Ancient Ones. But of late—since last spring—she has changed. Perhaps age has got the best of her. She no longer works the corn magic or burns the copal* . . ."

He glanced out the window and brightened. "What good fortune! There she is in the street outside. I will explain our plight. Perhaps just this one more time she will work the corn magic."

He dashed out, and I took advantage of the break to down two more aspirins from my dwindling supply. Then he was back, half-dragging, half-carrying a wizened little woman who was even more reluctant about our meeting than I.

Both were yelling, speaking far too fast for me to follow their Spanish, but their gestures told me what the argument was about. Paco was pointing in my direction and nodding vigorously. The *curadera* was pointing to me and shaking her head just as vehemently.

Whatever they might be saying, I approved of the woman's refusal to perform her magic on me. I made it a free-for-all, pointing at the *curadera* and nodding in my turn. "I'm with her."

Suddenly the little woman broke off her yelling. The silence was more deafening than the clamor. Paco and I watched, both a little apprehensive, as she came across the room toward me. Then I saw she was not looking at me but at my Bible open on the night stand.

Now she was pointing at a picture of Christ on the open page, groping visibly for her meager English. "You," she asked intensely, "you . . . Jesus?" I nodded, not fully comprehending.

Her smile washed over me like the breaking of floodgates. She placed both hands over her heart. "I . . . Jesus! I . . . Jesus!"

---

*Mixture of resins from tropical trees.

she kept repeating, tears rippling across the wrinkles in her face. I took her hands. The moisture in my own eyes was not from the head cold. Paco turned on his heel and strode out, muttering in complete frustration.

The little woman groped in the tattered folds of her dress to bring out a crumpled tract, worn almost threadbare from repeated handling. "Read!" she implored. I was thankful now for my years of high school Spanish that could permit me to come to at least a semblance of the correct pronunciation, even though I had to force the words past the burning in my throat.

My pronunciation didn't matter after all. She already knew every word of the tract by heart, and she mouthed them silently as I read, reveling in the hearing. The words were a simple telling about Christ and His Way to salvation.

"Where did you get this tract?" I asked.

With Guatemalan courtesy she turned back to the little English she knew. "Find," she gestured toward the boat dock. "Trash heap. American tourist, he read me." To these villagers, every "outsider" was a "tourist," even though few if any ever go there on vacation.

Suddenly her countenance clouded and she lapsed back into Spanish. "Forgive me! You are sick. I cannot work the corn magic any more. That is bad . . . evil. But I will pray. Jesus is good. He will take the sickness away."

She held my hand and prayed simply, with infinite trust, like a child asking Daddy to "fix."

"Thank you," I said, when she finished praying. I was surprised to note my voice wasn't as husky as it had been. When I swallowed, the fire in my throat wasn't quite so painful. *Wow, I thought, blindly, the aspirins are finally beginning to work.* Instantly I felt a nudge of rebuke. "She has more faith than you," a gentle Voice, not my own, said inside me.

In a flash of understanding I knew why, during my last flurry of packing, I had impulsively substituted my Spanish-language New Testament for my favorite one. I opened it now and began to read to her about the Christ she knew only from the meager verses on the tract. She was like a starved child, drinking in every word and pleading for "more . . . more . . ."

I had been reading most of the afternoon before I realized that the hoarseness and hurt had been steadily draining from my throat. The ache was going rapidly, too. As the fading light began to make reading difficult, I thrust the book into her hands. "Here, this is yours now. Jesus will always abide with you in His word."

She burst into tears. "But you are leaving! Who will read to me?"

"Is there no one in your village who can read?" I asked.

"Oh, there is the schoolmaster and one or two more. But they will not read to me. They are angry because I no longer cure them with corn magic. They do not want to know Jesus. They do not even want *me* to know Him."

I read one last verse to her, Acts 16:31. "Believe on the Lord Jesus Christ, and thou shalt be saved, and thy house."

Explaining that in this case I was sure the word *house* meant *village*, I urged her to go to the schoolmaster. "Ask him to read," I told her. "Then pray. The Lord will honor His word."

I did not see her again until two days later when I boarded the boat—on schedule and without my cold. When I turned for a last look at the village I saw two people standing hand in hand on the landing. They were the former village witch doctor and a young man who looked every inch a school-teacher. The radiance on both their faces told me what I didn't need to ask.

"See," I called back as the boat nosed into the river, "already your witness is doubled. You must not rest until all the village knows Him."

They both nodded eagerly and stood waving until the jungle underbrush closed in and blocked them from view. And all the way down the river my heart was singing in tune with the ripples. "Thank You, dear Heavenly Father, thank You for the happiest, most miserable cold You ever permitted me to have."

—*Vivienne L. George*

GOD USES HUMAN LOVE

*This is my commandment,
that you love one another
as I have loved you.*
—John 15:12, RSV

"Love lights the way." That familiar saying came true for one mother. While she lavished love on two lambs rejected by their dam, the barn around her filled with light that spilled out into the darkening farmyard. Another mother mourning the death of her son found that giving love away restored meaning to Christmas and brought an extra loving surprise from God.

Because God is love, when we act in love we are forming part of His circle that keeps love moving outward. Eventually, as a circle, it will return to us. We are also being God's daughters and sons, imitating the one who loved the world so much that He gave His Son—His only Son. We are being the light of the world.

Sometimes love doesn't get communicated before death. But as these stories show, it's never too late. Death is no barrier to God. One woman was thrilled to receive her father's "I love you" twenty years after his death.

For all of us, giving love is the most important thing we can do. And perhaps, as we give love to those around us, to those who need it, we ourselves will become part of His Mysterious Ways.

Kindness

Have you had a kindness shown?
  Pass it on;
'Twas not given for thee alone,
  Pass it on;
Let it travel down the years,
Let it wipe another's tears,
Till in Heaven the deed appears—
  Pass it on.

—*Henry Burton*

The Light in the Barn

I shoved the barn door open and yanked at the light chain. Only then did I remember. The bulb had burned out. I waited a moment until my eyes adjusted to the darkness and then made my way to the lambs' pen. In my hand I held a nursing bottle for two wobbly little creatures waiting for their dinner.

"Hi, guys," I said.

Two tiny tails leaped to life and eight little hooves scrambled across the straw. One lamb latched voraciously onto the bottle's nipple while the other bleated forlornly till it was his turn.

These were "bummer" lambs, twin males, and I was trying to save their lives. Their mother had rejected them at birth, not because they were twins, but because she had been unable to supply their milk.

When the bottle was drained, both lambs huddled next to me while I rubbed their stiff, curly coats. They seemed so content that I was reluctant to leave, so I just sat there in the dark cold, whispering sweet words, willing them strength, loving them for the mother who wouldn't. And then, in my cracked and uneven voice, I found myself singing, softly, as mothers have done down through the ages, my words half made up, a lullaby.

213

As I was on my way out of the barn, my husband, Jack, met me halfway.

"What kind of bulb did you put in there?" he asked.

"I didn't. It's still burned out."

"Did you have a lantern?"

I said no.

He looked at me quizzically. "When I came outside a few minutes ago, there was a light coming from the barn. It was bright, like sunshine, streaming out of every crack. It turned off just before you came out."

—Marjorie L. Smith

The Outcast

A chill ran through me as I was introduced to one of the inmates early in my first week as chaplain at the women's prison in Goochland, Virginia.

I tried to find something pleasant about the woman as she glared at me, but it was difficult. It was even hard to determine her age, for her face was horribly scarred and her hair was more wildcat than human.

The matron said Barbara was thirty-five, but her smouldering eyes reflected what seemed centuries of pent-up hate.

When I hesitantly stretched out my hand to shake hers, she eyed it with contempt, glared at me for a steely second, then spun around and strode back to her cell.

"Barbara's a bad one, I'm afraid," sighed Warden Kates. "She's considered hopeless for rehabilitation. Those face scars are from knifings, and that awful skin on her neck and arm is where a bucket of lye was thrown at her in a fight. She's so vicious that none of the other prisoners here will have anything to do with her."

She went on to tell how someone had made the mistake of sitting too close to Barbara one time in the dining hall, crowding her a bit. The adventurer leaped up screaming, blood streaming down her leg. It had been slit from ankle to knee with a stolen spoon Barbara had honed to razor sharpness on the cement floor of her cell.

I shuddered and wondered if this wasn't one prisoner I should avoid. Though I had attended Bible school and learned counseling techniques, I was fairly inexperienced and had never dealt with hardened criminals.

The next morning I heard sweeping outside my office. Through the window I saw it was Barbara. In a moment of boldness, I called out the window, "Good morning!"

She kept her head down, angrily slashing at the walk with the broom. "Ain't supposed to talk to no one while I'm workin'!" she snarled.

Forcing myself to continue, I said, "Well, I'll come to your cottage when you're finished."

"Forget it!" she snapped. "Nothin' to talk about." Then she was gone. *It's just as well,* I thought. I didn't know how to talk to someone like that. Maybe I had better leave well enough alone. All I could do, I felt, was to pray for her.

Yet something kept drawing me back to this sullen prisoner. A few days later I found myself looking up her record. As I read through the thick folder, I could well understand why everyone felt Barbara was hopeless.

I learned that she was now in prison for larceny. Because it was her third conviction, ten additional years—"Come back time" the girls call it—had been added to her basic sentence. Each of Barbara's former confinements in prisons around the state was documented with page after page of punishment reports for fighting, stealing, brewing "hooch," assaulting guards. I also noted that Barbara had no family on the outside. Her parents had disappeared when she was very young. After a succession of foster homes, there had been a stormy marriage that had ended in divorce.

In all of her folder, I failed to find one constructive element on which I could try to build a relationship.

"How does Barbara get along with the other girls?" I asked the matron of her cottage.

"Oh, she's hopeless!" she snorted. "There's no good in her at all. We just leave her alone and keep out of her way. It's a lot safer."

When I suggested that we might pray for Barbara, the matron laughed. "Me? Pray for *that* one? You won't catch me wasting my prayers on the likes of her!"

As I left the building, I felt my stubbornness flare. If the matron wouldn't help, I'd redouble my own prayers. Besides, wasn't Barbara the lost sheep that Jesus talked about, the one out of a hundred for whom we had to search through the rocky hills?

The next day I had a counseling session with Barbara. She sat in a chair by my desk like a trapped animal, head down, eyes darting toward the door.

Summoning up all my spiritual convictions and counseling training, I tried to reach this lonely soul trapped within the scarred, tormented body.

"Barbara, do you know that God loves you?"

"Ain't nobody loves me!" Her hands twisted together in her lap.

"Jesus gave His life for us so that we could start new lives for ourselves."

She spat on the floor and looked up at me, glaring. "Don't want none of that preachin' stuff. It's all words . . . don't mean a thing!" She got up and headed for the door.

A few times after that I'd try to speak to her while she was doing chores. But she would keep her head down as she swept, or would glare at me in hate. Discouraged, I found myself beginning to avoid her. I justified this with the thought that some people really are hopeless. "Lord," I sighed, "I give up. I leave her to You."

But though I stayed away from Barbara, something I had seen deep in those dark eyes continued to haunt me.

I joined the prisoners out on the lawn one hot summer day during recreation time. Then I noticed Barbara. As usual she was standing apart from the others. The heat felt like a blanket, and I thought how readily my pale Canadian skin burned in this fierce southern sun. The other girls were strolling and talking, but Barbara stood alone, motionless. As I looked at her, my eyes were drawn to her scarred throat, bare where the collar of her blouse was turned back. Her skin there looked so thin and tightly drawn.

Oh, I thought, *how that poor skin must burn when she gets too much sun on it. It looks so sensitive . . .*

Suddenly I remembered that somewhere in my belongings was a soft, pink silk handkerchief. Back in my room I rum-

maged until I found it, along with two gold-colored pins. I
hesitated. Then I forced myself to walk casually outside toward
Barbara.

When she saw me coming, it took all my determination to
keep going in her direction. I could see the anger seething in
her dark eyes. The matron's words echoed in my memory: *We
keep out of her way. It's a lot safer.*

"Barbara," I said, my voice trembling in spite of myself,
"this sun is burning me up. And your neck looks so sensitive.
Would you let me pin this little piece of silk on the neckline
of your blouse to protect you from the sun?"

My words sounded foolish to me. They must have sounded
strange to Barbara, too, judging from her look of confusion.
But I tried to ignore her clenched fists as I held out the little
pink square of silk. Silently praying for courage, I took the
final step, reached up and laid the tiny handkerchief across her
throat. With fumbling fingers I fastened it in place with the
pins.

Barbara said nothing, but two tears welled up in her dark
eyes to run down her scarred cheeks and moisten the square
of pink. Except for that, her face was as stony as ever. She
stamped her foot, gritted her teeth and, knuckling her tears
away, spat on the ground.

I turned away from her and sought the shelter of my office.
Have I made any contact? I wondered. *Is this a beginning?* A
Scripture buried in my memory reminded me that when God
begins a work, He can be counted on to finish it. I kept
praying, "Lord, don't let me scare her off now. Please guide
me by Your Spirit."

A few days later I was prompted to contact Barbara again.
This time, as she sat in my office, I didn't try to lead her into
the plan of salvation. I just told her that I wanted to be her
friend.

She glanced at me warily. "Why?"

I didn't have the words to answer. Then I remembered my
own loneliness, growing up in a family of younger sisters and
brothers who seemed so much more attractive and accom-
plished than I was. I reached out to touch Barbara's hand, then
thought better of it. I just said, "Because I know how it is to
have no friends."

For an instant a spark of understanding flickered in her eyes. As the months went by I kept trying to get through to Barbara. Sometimes she would seem receptive. We talked of our lives, disappointments and hopes. I told her how I had been confined to bed for eight years with arthritis that was considered incurable.

"How come you got better?"

"Jesus . . . the Lord Jesus healed me."

Then at our next meeting she would be gone again, retreating into herself like an animal burrowing into the corner of its cage.

But I kept trying to let Barbara know in little ways that she was loved.

Then one morning her matron gave me a note. It was tearsplotched, the crude spelling all but indecipherable, but as nearly as I could tell, the note said: "Chaplain, I ain't slept all night. You better get down here right away."

I ran to Barbara's cell. She was lying on her cot, staring at the ceiling with eyes red and swollen. When I entered the room, she flung herself at me and burst into sobbing that shook her whole frame. I hugged her, praying, rejoicing because I knew what had happened. Through the months, the gentle urging of His Spirit had finally penetrated Barbara's heart. She had opened the door and let Him in. The vicious, hardened criminal had died. In its place was a new creature, awash with God's love. The little square of pink silk was pinned to her pillow.

From then on Barbara was a different person. Not only were her chores done quickly and efficiently, but she began searching for educational courses to take in her free time. "I know I don't speak too good," she confessed to me.

She spent a lot of time reading the Bible, and helped me in little ways.

Months later, completely rehabilitated, she was released, a poised, alert, almost handsome woman. Now I found myself filling out recommendations for her for Bible schools and later for jobs in nursing homes. Eventually, she became a county supervisor of all the nursing homes for the elderly in a large midwestern state.

Recently, I opened one of my friend Barbara's letters to find a photo showing her holding in her still lye-scarred arms a tiny elderly lady with a halo of white hair around a wrinkled face glowing with joy.

"This little old lady had no faith or hope," wrote Barbara, "but now she does. She's looking to Jesus for all her needs, just as I keep looking to Him for all of mine."

My tears moistened the letter and my heart felt as if it would burst with joy. If God could use a little scrap of silk to begin such a transformation in a hopeless person, then surely there is hope for all the world.

—Kay Golbeck

Prayer for the Helpless

Let me be a voice for the speechless,
Those who are small and weak;
Let me speak for all helpless creatures
Who have no power to speak.
I have lifted my heart to heaven
On behalf of the least of these—
The frightened, the homeless, the hungry.
I am voicing their pleas.
If I can help any creature,
Respond to a desperate call,
I will know that my prayer has been answered
By the God Who created them all.

—Helen Inwood

When I Stood in Margie's Place

One day during World War II, I held a letter from my father that said, "Mother is in the hospital awaiting surgery. She wishes that you could be with her."

But there I was, half a world away in a field hospital on the battlegrounds of France. General George Patton's tanks were pushing toward Metz. The casualties were heavy. A steady stream of ambulances linked the broken roads. Our tents overflowed with praying, cursing and deadly quiet men.

One of the mortally wounded men reached out to me. "Are you there, Margie? Hold my hand."

I was not Margie, but the failing vision and clouded mind of this soldier let him think I was. I do not know who "Margie" was—wife, sister, sweetheart—but she was obviously greatly loved and very important to him.

"Are you still there, Margie? Don't go away," pleaded the man. My hand tightened on his weakening grasp, and I whispered, "I'll stay with you—always."

As I stood beside the drab-blanketed cot holding a stranger's hand whose life was ebbing, my thoughts spanned the ocean—to my mother in the hospital. And there came to me suddenly the overwhelming conviction that some stranger in that hospital was comforting her, too.

Some days later a letter came from my parents in which they spoke lovingly of a certain nurse who had "adopted" mother, a nurse who said, "I'll take care of things here. Tell your daughter to look after things over there."

It is beyond one's power to pay back in kind and to the same person each debt of love we owe. But we can pass on to others a service or a kindness wherever we see the need, and help make the world a little more gentle and warm.

—*Elizabeth Mulligan*

When Christ Came Back into Christmas

Our oldest son had died early in December. Numb with grief, my husband, Fred, and I thought a trip to Florida might help, but it didn't. As we drove north toward home, I began to pray. "Father, I know we can't have our son back, but could You somehow bring *Your* Son back into our Christmas? We need Him so!"

Just after we crossed the Georgia state line we passed a couple standing by the road, hoping, I supposed, for a ride. "Did that woman have a *baby?*" I asked Fred. We backed up and motioned the trio into the car. The man was small, his wife very young, the baby pale and quiet. They were migrant workers, the man told us. "Our baby girl taken sick," he said. "Then *she* taken sick. Medicine and clinic took all my money."

"Are they all right?" I asked worriedly.

"They're okay. But there's just no way of making it like we were doing. I got a friend in Tennessee owns trucks. I can drive a truck real good. He might could give me a job."

The car radio had reported snow in Tennessee. Fred and I glanced at each other and nodded in agreement. We pulled into a motel and invited the family to be our guests for the night. After supper we arranged for the man to telephone his friend to ask if a job possibility really existed. It did.

The next day we drove the family to the bus depot in Athens, Georgia, and bought tickets for them. I felt more at peace than I had for many days. And then, when the woman turned to say good-bye, I knew why. "We sure do thank you," she said. "And so does Christine." It was the first time I'd heard the baby's name.

—*Closs Peace Wardlaw*

The Music Box

My hobby is collecting music boxes—nothing expensive or rare or old, just music boxes I like and enjoy listening to. For years my mother's favorite was a figurine of an old woman sitting in a rocking chair and holding a few balloons.

Every time my mother came to visit me, she would go into the den and look at the music box and smile thoughtfully. Then she'd say, "If Pa goes first, that's me—sitting on a rocking chair in Lincoln Park, selling balloons." We would laugh. Then she would push the button and listen to the song it played—"Try to Remember" from *The Fantasticks.*

In 1970, Mother, then approaching eighty, suffered a mild stroke that put her in the hospital for a week. After that, she never became completely well again. Gradually her weakness increased. My father, who had been retired for several years, now became Mother's constant attendant. My sister and I took turns going over there one day a week to shop, clean house and prepare casseroles and stews that my father could warm up for their meals.

Often my mother would ask me, "How's the old lady with the balloons?"

"Fine," I'd say. "She asks about you all the time." And we'd laugh.

In October 1974, my phone rang very early one morning. It was my father. He said, "Honey, you'd better get over here. It's Ma."

"What happened?" I asked, fearing the worst.

"She fell getting out of bed," he said. "I don't have the strength to lift her."

"I'll be right there," I said. I called my sister, told her the bad news and said I'd pick her up on the way.

We found Mother sitting on the floor in her room, resting against her bed. Her face was sad and helpless, with tears of humiliation in her eyes. We got her back in bed.

"I'm sorry this happened," she whispered. "Thanks for coming. I'll make it up to you."

Those were her last words to us.

I called the doctor. An ambulance was there in minutes, but on the way to the hospital Mother lost consciousness. She was put into intensive care. While out in the waiting room the doctor told us, "It's very bad. There's been a lot of brain damage. She may not come out of this."

It was the beginning of a long ordeal for all of us. Mother went into a coma. Ten days later she was transferred to a private room where we could stay with her all day. Dad left the room frequently for a cigarette, his pain a constant frown on his face.

I was there every day, all day. Mother remained in a coma but I talked to her anyway hoping she could somehow hear me. "We're all praying for you, Ma," I told her, "everybody— even the old lady with the balloons."

Early in the morning on November 19, with our house still in darkness, the phone rang. I braced myself. "Hello?"

"Mrs. Miller, this is the head nurse at the hospital. I'm sorry to have to tell you that your mother died ten minutes ago."

Even though I had been expecting them, her words were like a blow. "Thank you," I managed to say somehow. "I'll take care of everything." As I hung up, I glanced at the clock. It was 5:10 A.M. My mother had died at 5:00, after being in a coma for forty-nine days.

Somehow we all got through the next few days. Then came the strain of adjusting to the loss, of waiting for the sorrow to fade. Time passed, but the sorrow did not disappear. When death takes a loved one, even though you trust in the promise of everlasting life, something in you longs for reassurance, for proof of that promise. It's only human, I guess.

The months went by. One season slipped into another. One day, my husband, Lenny, came home from work with a bad cold. I suggested that he spend a couple of days in bed, but he said he had too much work to do at the office and couldn't spare the time. A few days later, the cold was so bad that he had no choice. I nursed him all day, and then, so he could sleep undisturbed, I spent the night on the sofa in the den.

It had been a hard day for me, because it was the day before the first anniversary of Mother's death. I kept thinking about her, missing her, wishing she were only a telephone call away. It would have been so helpful just to talk to her, ask her advice about Lenny, feel the warmth and reassurance she always gave.

Tired and worried about Lenny, I tossed fitfully on the sofa for a while. I kept thinking about all the uncertainties of life, and I felt lost and lonely somehow. I missed our familiar bed and Lenny's comforting presence. Finally I drifted off into a restless sleep.

Hours later I woke with a start; something strange, something unfamiliar had wakened me. For a moment I didn't know what it was. Then I heard the music. The soft sounds of a familiar song drifted through my mind. But where was it coming from? There was darkness all around me. Had I been dreaming it? No, the music was still playing. In the darkness I could still hear its eerie tinkling.

I sat up. I stared into the gloom. There, on the desk, was the silhouette of the old lady with the balloons, and the song I heard coming from the music box was my mother's favorite, "Try to Remember."

"But it can't be playing," I said to myself. "Nobody's touched it. And the last time I played that box I distinctly remember letting it run down!"

And then I remembered what day it was. November 19. I glanced at the desk clock. It was 5:00 A.M. Ma had died exactly one year ago to the day, to the hour, to the minute! I began to cry. I whispered to the dark: "If that's you, Ma, I hope you're safe and happy. You know that we still love you and miss you and, yes, we still remember."

I lay down again, weeping, listening to the music until it stopped, and I fell asleep, reassured at last.

I awoke again around 7:30 and smelled bacon. I got up and went to the kitchen. There was Lenny, shaved, fully dressed, at the stove frying bacon and eggs. "You were so sound asleep that I decided to fix breakfast myself," he said. "I'm going to work."

I stared at him, astonished. "Are you well enough for that?"

"Yes," he said. "During the night the cold just seemed to melt out of me. I feel great."

I felt as if I were going to cry again. "I'll do that," I said. I took the spatula away from Lenny and turned my back to him, close to tears.

Lenny went to the table and sat down to his cup of coffee. He said, "Tell me something. Did I hear you playing Ma's music box during the night or did I dream it?"

I fought the tears. I couldn't talk about it yet.

"No," I said. "I didn't play it."

And in my heart I thanked the Lord for using a little mechanical music box to let us know that our mother was safe with Him, that she still loved us, still missed us, and, yes, still remembered.

—*Shirley Miller*

Uncle Wilson's Last Words

In September 1983 Uncle Wilson, my mother's only brother, underwent surgery for an intestinal tumor. The doctors, discovering a tumor too large and complex to remove, gave him from four to six months to live. Uncle Wilson was brought home to spend his remaining days. With no wife to see to his needs, his care fell to my mother, her two sisters and us nieces and nephews.

We all worked hard to make Uncle Wilson comfortable, but he was bedridden, helpless and in great pain. Day after day we tended to his needs, tried to soothe his fears. And every night before bed I knelt and asked God to heal this good, kind man.

In July 1984, ten hard months having passed, Uncle Wilson took a turn for the worse. I was called and told to come at once. I stood by his bed, waiting for the rescue squad ambulance to come, and even in his pain Uncle Wilson tried to communicate his love and thanks by kissing my hand.

By now I was no longer praying for his healing, but simply asking that God take my uncle to be with Him. And then, early in the morning of his third day in the hospital, my sister and I were with him when Uncle Wilson suddenly opened his eyes, and in a loud and clear voice he cried, "My God! My God! My God!" My sister and I were wonderstruck.

Uncle Wilson died soon after, but my family was sustained by his words. My uncle, you see, had been deaf and mute since birth. These words were the first he had ever spoken.

—*Margaret Murray*

The First to Know

My husband, Ollie, had retired from teaching and we were making plans to spend time in Florida, to travel, to relish our time together. Then a devastating illness struck and Ollie was left weak and gaunt, hardly able to speak. Weeks passed and it became clear that Ollie was near death. We held tight to our faith.

Someone was always in Ollie's hospital room—either I was there or our grown children, Bruce and Karen; sometimes our pastor. One day, in his faltering speech, Ollie told our son, "Go home, Bruce . . . you should be with Gwen."

Bruce lived many miles away and his wife was about to have a baby. We felt an extra sadness, knowing Ollie would never see his first grandchild.

"I don't want to leave you, Dad," Bruce protested.

"You belong . . . with Gwen."

Reluctantly, Bruce left. "When the baby comes," he said to Ollie, "you'll be the first to know."

A few days later, around two in the afternoon, Ollie awoke from a nap. He turned and looked at me. I leaned close to hear his halting words. "The baby . . . is coming now . . . it's . . . a boy." For an instant the old sparkle was in his eyes as he smiled at what he saw. Then he dozed again.

I had sent Karen home to rest, but soon she was back. "Bruce called," she told me. "Gwen went into labor around two o'clock."

That night, peacefully, Ollie died. A few hours later, his first grandchild was born. A healthy baby boy.

Ollie had been the first to know.

—*M. J. Gardner*

"You Should See What I'm Seeing"

Springtime in Washington, cherry blossom time. When that wonderful sea of pink blossoms foams along our capital's avenues, I always wish everyone in the world could see it. And one year I did invite my parents to come down from Cape May, New Jersey, and visit me at cherry blossom time, but word came back that health problems made such a trip impossible.

Then, on the very day when I had hoped they could be with me, I had a telephone call at the office, telling me that my mother had just died.

I sat there stunned with disbelief and shock. Finally I organized my office work after a fashion, told my coworkers that I would be gone for a week, and walked down the stairs of the U.S. Naval Oceanographic Office. As I reached the street, I was trembling, overwhelmed by the terrible sense of grief and loss. Somehow I made my way to my car and put my keys in the ignition. And as I did I heard Mother's voice say quite clearly and distinctly, "Oh, Audre, if you think the cherry blossoms are beautiful, you should see what I'm seeing!"

Then I cried, but in joy as well as sorrow.

—*Audre L. Tribbe*

The Legacy of Mary Elizabeth

Sarah Bird was nearly eighty-six, but her eyes were bright and her mind alert. When I visited her in the Home for the Aged here in St. Cloud, Florida, she reminisced about days gone by, as if talking about them would bring closer the friends and loved ones now gone or separated by distance. Here is one story she told me that has lived in my mind ever since . . .

Sarah Bird was born on a farm about three miles south of Baldwinsville, New York. She married the boy next door and the young couple moved with proper ceremony into a home given them by her parents. "Come joy or sorrow, we know that God is head of this home," her husband declared.

At first there was mostly sorrow. Their first baby, a boy, died before he was two. Then little Mary Elizabeth was born and brought much joy. She was a strong and healthy child until she developed heart trouble after a siege of pneumonia at the age of five. For the last few years of her life, Mary Elizabeth lay in her little brass bed in her own brightly furnished room at the head of the stairs.

The child spent much time reading. Once, when a picture of four little orphaned sisters appeared in the local paper, Mary Elizabeth asked a special favor of her father. "Would you please go to the orphanage and buy them for me? I have eight dollars. Please, Daddy. That one little girl has the same name as me—Mary Elizabeth."

But the father had to say no, explaining that with the cook-ing for the two hired men, the care of her blind grandmother and all the other work, it would be too much for her mother. Time passed.

When she was nine, life slowly ebbed away. Somehow Mary Elizabeth knew what was happening. But she showed no fear. Instead, she had one final request. Would her father please buy a baby girl at the orphanage because her mommy would be so lonesome when she left? The baby was to have blue eyes like the sky outside her window.

With heavy heart, her father gave her his solemn promise.

Mary Elizabeth died on Maundy Thursday, and on Easter Sunday was laid to rest in the little cemetery nearby. Weeks later, her father at last told his wife of his promise.

"It would be too much to care for an infant," Mrs. Bird said, still grief-stricken. "I'm busy from dawn until far into the evening."

"But I gave Mary Elizabeth my word," her husband said. "We could hire someone to help you."

They visited the orphanage, made an application for adop-tion and went home to wait for their baby. Two months later the call came; the baby was ready to be taken home. It was a beautiful infant, just six weeks old, but it had brown eyes! The man remembered his promise that it be a blue-eyed baby. Was there one?

The orphanage director admitted there was another child, a blue-eyed girl, eighteen months old. "She is rather sickly, and screams whenever a man comes near her," she added.

The child was named Adelaide. The director would bring her down for Mrs. Bird to see, but perhaps her husband wouldn't mind stepping to the back of the room?

He did so. But Adelaide saw him right away. Her thin arms stretched out to him, and when he held her, she smiled. They took her home that very day.

After a month, Adelaide looked like a different child. Sun-shine and good country food put weight on the frail little body and in six months she was healthy and happy. On several occasions the orphanage director visited the farm to see how little Adelaide was getting along. During one of these calls, she asked Mrs. Bird if she would grant her a favor.

"There is a very unusual nine-year-old girl at the orphanage who has never been on a farm," she told Mrs. Bird. "Could you possibly take her for a weekend visit? Her name is Mary Elizabeth."

Remembering her own Mary Elizabeth, Mrs. Bird agreed to take the girl but only for the weekend. On Friday evening the little girl arrived, looking very forlorn, very lost and very subdued in her somber orphanage clothes. Even though she was staying only two days, the couple decided to pretty her up. On Saturday they took her shopping and bought her an entire new outfit: pretty black lace stockings to replace her heavy ribbed ones, and slippers with bows, a new blue coat with a hat to match and a dress trimmed with yards of lace. The child stood in front of the mirror at the farmhouse, her hands lovingly caressing the lace, her eyes alive with joy.

Over the weekend, Mary Elizabeth joined the household routine. She insisted on helping with the dusting, making the beds and playing with little Adelaide. Then Monday morning came and the lady from the orphanage arrived to take her back to the home.

Mary Elizabeth stood at the door with the box of new clothing under her arm. She smiled at Mrs. Bird, thanked her and asked wistfully, "I didn't make good here either, did I?"

"We told you it was only for a weekend visit," the lady from the orphanage explained.

Mary Elizabeth didn't answer. As she turned to go, Mrs. Bird could see the tears trickling down her face.

"It stabbed my heart," Sarah Bird said. "We couldn't let her go." Within a few weeks the adoption papers were in order, and Mary Elizabeth joined the family. In fact, she moved right into the room at the head of the stairs that had always been kept just as Mrs. Bird's own little Mary Elizabeth had left it—twin dolls sitting up in the corner, her favorite toys neatly arranged on the shelves alongside her book of Bible stories and scrapbooks.

One rainy Saturday afternoon when Mrs. Bird was mixing molasses cookies in the kitchen, the little girl asked if she could look at the scrapbooks. She promised to put them back just as she found them, for she knew that the room was very special to her new mother.

The second batch of cookie dough was rolled out on the board ready to be cut when the child ran down the stairs shouting:

"Mother, Mother, your Mary Elizabeth has my picture in her scrapbook!"

Mrs. Bird tried to convince the youngster that it couldn't be. Her own little girl had passed away nearly four years before and had no way of knowing her. But the child insisted:

"Yes, she did. She wanted me. She picked me out!"

Mrs. Bird wiped her floured hands on her long apron and went to the foot of the stairs. The child brought down the old scrapbook and, there, pasted on one of the last pages, was the newspaper clipping with pictures of four little orphaned sisters. Circled in crayon was the oldest one—Mary Elizabeth.

I'll never forget Sarah Bird's radiant face as she finished her story: "I was convinced then that my own little girl had indeed sent me both the blue-eyed baby Adelaide and the second Mary Elizabeth. They were like gifts from heaven."

—*Theresa Budinger*

Dad's Lodge Ring

My dad was frugal about some things—wouldn't spend much on himself. For instance, though he was devoted to his lodge, he wouldn't indulge in a lodge ring. But his love for his children—my brother Bob especially—was extravagant.

When World War II broke out, my handsome, fearless brother became a Marine fighter pilot. Early in 1944, he died under enemy fire in the South Pacific.

Mother's faith sustained her, but my father aged before our eyes. He began missing work. He lost interest in everything, and even stopped going to his lodge meetings.

As Christmas approached, Mother and I worried even more about Dad. The holiday had been Bob's favorite. His Christmas surprises were legendary—a dollhouse made at school for me, a puppy hidden away for little brother, an expensive dress for Mother bought with the first money he ever earned.

Dad's grief continued to drain his strength. Mother and I prayed together. "Dear God, help us through Christmas."

On December 23, an official-looking package arrived— more of Bob's personal effects returned by the government. Dad watched grimly as Mother unwrapped Bob's dress uniform. As she refolded it to pack it away, she automatically went through the pockets. "What's this?" she murmured suddenly. Then, with a little cry, she handed it to Dad.

I'll never forget the look that transformed his face—a blend of wonder, hope and healing, as if Bob were still with us.

In his hand, he held a neatly folded fifty dollar bill with a note in Bob's handwriting: "For Dad's lodge ring."

—Mary Sherman Hilbert

Danny's Dad

"Stay away from the pool, Danny," I told my three-year-old as he headed for the backyard to ride his Big Wheel.

"Yes, Mom," he said obediently.

Listening to the sound of his plastic tricycle, I returned to the kitchen, sighing. It was not easy being a widow, and raising two children on my own was often a strain.

I busied myself about the house until something made me stop dead still. I cocked my ear. No sounds of Danny's tricycle.

I rushed to the kitchen window and looked out at the swimming pool. Danny's Big Wheel was bobbing in the water, and there, floating face down, was Danny.

Desperately I pulled Danny out of the water and tried to administer CPR, but his body was cold and his face was gray. Then the sirens, the paramedics, the helicopter whisking Danny off to the hospital, where he lay in a coma. Finally, after my long, prayerful vigil, Danny opened his eyes. Soon he was well again, back home playing as usual. But somehow he seemed changed.

One day he blurted out, "Mom, I want to see a picture of my daddy." I had not realized I had never shown him a picture of his father, who had died before Danny was born. The first photograph I brought out showed my husband and his baseball team.

Danny looked at it for a few moments. Then he pointed to one of the coaches.

"That's my daddy," he said.

"How do you know?" I asked.

"He talked to me in the hospital before I woke up. He said, 'You must go home now. Mommy needs you.' "

I looked at the man he'd pointed to; it was the father he had never seen.

—*Cathy Slack*
as told to *Skip Westphal*

Words from the Past

My father was a very reserved Canadian of English origin. Though he was a sensitive, loving parent, he wasn't a man to express his deepest feelings. Dad died almost twenty years ago, but often since, I've felt a twinge of yearning . . . I didn't remember him ever saying "I love you."

Recently, my son asked me to show him how to letter a title on the folder for a school assignment. "Oh, I wish your grandfather was here," I exclaimed, shaking my head. "He had an unusual way of lettering his blueprints. He even showed me how simple it was to do. But I've forgotten the trick of it."

For hours afterward, I racked my brain, trying to remember how Dad formed those simple, distinctive letters; but all I could summon up was a nostalgic image of him bending over his drawing board.

The next day my brother stopped by unexpectedly. He handed me a worn, folded envelope. "I was helping Mother sort through some of Dad's old papers, and we found this. Looks like something Dad must have done for you. We thought you'd like to have it."

When I unfolded the envelope, I felt a shiver of excitement. On it before me, in Dad's special lettering, was a complete alphabet, the very one I'd wanted to show my son.

It was like a message sent from Heaven.

But even more thrilling was the notation at the bottom in my father's familiar hand—"This what you want, Dot?" And, alongside it, framed in a diamond, three words, words that were a long time in the coming, but not too late to warm me for the rest of my life.

"I love you."

—Dorothy Corson

Last Chance

Have you ever felt bad enough to want to take your own life? Probably not. But I have. And I can tell you: It's not a pleasant feeling.

I'm a Chicano, raised in Southern California. I dropped out of school when I was thirteen, became a dope user and then a pusher, was arrested sixteen times and hated everybody. When I could get a job, it was dirty and low-paying. I was angry all the time; I thought every man was either a potential enemy to be feared or a potential sheep to be fleeced. I even hated God.

When I was sixteen I married, and soon Cherry and I had three children. But I couldn't take care of them, and when I went to prison they nearly starved.

Once when Cherry was pregnant with our third child, she came to visit me at San Bernardino County Prison Camp. It shocked me to see how sick she looked.

"You better go to the doctor," I said through the wire grate that separated us.

She shook her head. "There's no money, Tino, not even for milk."

This was before the days of widespread public welfare, and there was no one we could turn to for help. But I made Cherry promise she'd see the doctor anyway. You can't imagine how helpless I felt. It seemed like life was an endless journey for which I had lost the map. I was enraged yet powerless—so I prayed. Sort of.

"God, You've got to help her," I muttered angrily after she'd gone. "I can't." But I expected nothing.

The next time Cherry came she looked better. She'd had the flu, but the doctor had given her medicine and had also sent an order to the grocer's to deliver two quarts of milk a day and a loaf of bread.

I despised his charity.

When I got out of prison, things went a little better for about a year. I got a job doing yard work—just enough to keep us going. But soon things began to slide. I got drunk. I was still on morphine. I couldn't hold a job. I shouted at the kids and lied to Cherry. When I got depressed, I cried and told them that I was the worst husband and father on earth. I despised myself.

One afternoon, in a severe drug depression, I went home. Cherry was in the living room ironing and the kids were playing on the floor. She ignored me as I stumbled in.

"Can't you even say hello?" I said.

Her eyes filled with tears. "Tino, why are you doing this to yourself? To us?"

"Doing what?" I yelled. "It's not my fault I can't get a job."

Cherry's face went cold and the kids started to cry. They cowered away from me. My own kids.

You're ruining their lives, I thought. Right then and there the thought came to me that the one thing I could do for my family was to kill myself and get out of their lives for good. I had a little insurance policy and that would help them more than I could. I slammed the door and ran out to my car. I didn't need a map to show me where I was going. I was going to the end of the road.

We'd had a lot of rain that sp ring, and the mountain roads were muddy. I figured it would be easy to slide over the edge of a cliff, and the coroner would just say it was "failure to negotiate a curve." So I headed for the rugged hills above San Bernardino. I was in a state of despair. My head felt like a hollow drum; my legs would hardly obey me. When I passed through a little town just before dark, I decided to stop for a last drink because my courage was getting shaky.

I went into a little general store. The storekeeper said he

didn't have any beer. He was alone. It occurred to me that I could hit him over the head and clean out the cash register. But then I thought, *What difference would that make?*

"Got some root beer, though," the storekeeper said. "Nice and cold. I make it myself, and it's real good, if I do say so. Here, let me give you a taste and see if you don't like it." He was a cheerful old coot. One of those salt-of-the-earth types that I'd always thought were saps.

He clinked ice into a glass, poured the brown liquid from a jug in the cooler and held it out to me with a smile. I took a sip. It *was* good, but I was struck more by the warmth and openness of the man. I wasn't used to it. Whenever someone was friendly to me, I always asked myself, *What does he want?*

I drank the root beer and put the glass on the counter. I wanted to get away and get on with my business.

"Going up in the mountains?" he asked. "Wish I could get away. There's something about a mountain that gives you a better look at things, isn't there? Yes," he went on, "I often think of the Psalm: 'I will lift up mine eyes unto the hills' " (121:1).

Whenever I heard Bible talk, I usually tightened up. But this old guy was going right on.

"You know they used to print that with a comma after it, followed by 'from whence cometh my help,' and I liked to think of help coming from the mountains. But in this Bible"— he pulled out the book from under the counter as quick as someone drawing a gun, so quick that I jumped—"there's a period after 'hills' and a question mark after the next part, so it reads: 'I lift up my eyes to the hills. From whence does my help come? My help comes from the Lord.' And I guess that makes more sense, doesn't it?"

"I never thought of it," I muttered. God had never concerned Himself with me, so I never concerned myself with Him.

"Well, I think about it every day," the storekeeper continued. "When you came in, I was feeling kind of lonesome. My wife usually helps me in the store, but she's gone to be with our daughter when she has her baby, and I have to go home to an empty house."

He hesitated. "Say, if you haven't anything better to do, why not come on home with me for supper? My wife fixed up a stew yesterday before she left. How about it?"

"Thanks, but . . ."

"You got a wife and kids at home, I'll bet. You look like a good family man."

His words seemed to touch a raw nerve. "I'm not!" I burst out. "I'm not a good family man at all! I'm a rotten husband and a worse father. I'm nothing! You've probably never known a person like me before. I've robbed, taken drugs, been in prison almost as many years as I've been out. When I came in here, I thought of knocking you out and robbing the store. You want to know what I'm really doing here? All right, I'll tell you!"

I found the words pouring out of me to this stranger in a way I'd never talked to anyone in my whole life. I told him everything. He didn't say much; he wasn't scared or disgusted; he nodded a few times as if he understood, and then handed me the Bible. It was open to the book of Philippians.

"Begin right here." He pointed to verse thirteen of chapter four. "Read that sentence."

And I read, " 'I can do all things in him who strengthens me' " (RSV).

"But I can't do anything," I whispered.

"That's right, you can't—but Christ the Lord can. It's true, you know. God is with you all the time. I think He was responsible for your stopping here this afternoon. You thought it was just to get one last drink, but God was giving you one last chance. Won't you give Him a chance to help you turn your life around? What do you have to lose by taking Him at His word?"

What did I have to lose? Nothing. I had nothing.

I repeated the phrase, letting the meaning sweep through me. "I can do *all things* . . ." Even conquer the drug habit? If only that were true! I looked into the storekeeper's kind face, and suddenly a great happiness filled the emptiness of despair. I kept repeating those wonderful words of assurance: "I can do all things in him who strengthens me." Could I? Could He? I found myself weeping.

When I left that little store near San Bernardino, the store-keeper gave me his own Bible. I went home.

Cherry was standing at the kitchen table. When the kids saw me, they ran behind her. There was my family staring at me like I was an intruder.

"What do you want now?" Cherry asked warily.

"I want to come home," I said. I saw her questioning look.

"Look, kids," I said, "a man gave me something on my trip today. Want to see it?"

They were hesitant, but I took out the Book and showed them.

"What is it?" Cherry asked.

"A road map. It showed me the way home."

It's a map I'm still following today. And every day.

—*Tino Carrasco*

Prayer for Those Unheard

Lord, bless me with a listening mind.
Attune me to the smaller sounds,
The whispered plea of loneliness,
The whimper of an unloved child.

The sad, the sick, the lost. All these
Ignored, unheard by passersby.
And use me, Lord, to meet their needs
That I may, in a Christlike way,
Reflect Thy love for them each day.

—*Irene Sharp*

A Circle of Love

India Albery was, perhaps, the most unusual person ever to work at Guideposts. Lady Albery—for that was her title—

seldom spoke about herself. We knew only that she had come from England, that her early life had been privileged, but that when she first came to Guideposts, she was old and alone and impoverished, living in a shabby room with a few cherished keepsakes.

She met adversity bravely, but with a stern and haughty demeanor. I myself tried hard, but I could not break through her British reserve. I used to pray that I'd find some way to reach her, but she was too proud to let any emotion show.

One lunch hour in December, I was browsing in an antique shop, a favorite pastime. I seldom purchased anything, but this day was different. I spied an enamel pencil in a silver case. It had a large "A" in its elaborate monogram and I felt an urging—almost a physical nudge—to buy it for Lady Albery.

"What's this?" she asked brusquely when I handed her the tiny package.

"Just a little Christmas something," I said apprehensively.

When Lady Albery opened the package and saw the silver case, her body tensed, and her eyes filled with tears. "Dina," she said—never before had she used my first name—"Dina, how did you know?"

"Know what?" I asked.

"This once belonged to me," she said. "I had to sell it years ago, when I was hungry and desperate. It was given to me by someone I loved. And now your kindness has brought it back."

A circle of love, I thought, *I've been part of a circle of love.*

And Lady Albery never forgot it.

—*Dina Donohue*